THE
PROPHETIC
VOICE

GARRIS ELKINS

The Prophetic Voice
© 2016 Garris Elkins

Prophetic Horizons
PO Box 509, Jacksonville, OR, 97530 USA
info@prophetichorizons.com | www.GarrisElkins.com

ISBN: 0692530118
ISBN-13: 978-0692530115

DEDICATION

I dedicate this book to the Church. You are a prophetic community; may you rise to the fullness of the prophetic mantle God has placed upon your life. I dedicate this book to those within the Church who are just beginning to sense the first stirring of prophecy; may you hunger for more. I dedicate this book to those of you who have walked in this gift for many years as a seasoned prophetic voice; may you challenge yourself to finish well in the strength of humility. To each of you, no matter where God has assigned you to live and minister, you are a critical component in the plan of God. May you speak with Spirit-empowered courage to a world waiting to hear the message of hope transmitted within the unique sound of your voice.

CONTENTS

FOREWORD 1

PREFACE 3

INTRODUCTION 5

Chapter 1: The Power of Encounter 10

Prophetic Principle: A Promised Breakthrough 14

Chapter 2: A Sudden Deposit 15

Prophetic Principle: The Voice of Humility 20

Chapter 3: Delayed Delivery 21

Prophetic Principle: Dealing With Pushback 24

Chapter 4: Revealing Hidden Things 26

Prophetic Principle: When to Remain Silent 28

Chapter 5: Inquire of the Lord 30

Prophetic Principle: Prophesying Into Dark Places ... 34

Chapter 6: Prophetic Alignment 36

Prophetic Principle: Resist the Urge 38

Chapter 7: Words That Redefine 40

Prophetic Principle: Don't Take It Personally 45

Chapter 8: Declaring the Mysteries of Heaven ... 46

*Prophetic Principle: Prophesying Hope to the Next
Generation* 50

Chapter 9: Changing History 51

Prophetic Principle: When You Said Too Much 55

Chapter 10: Navigating Correction 57

Prophetic Principle: Challenging Territory 60

Chapter 11: The Power of a Single Word 62

Prophetic Principle: Delayed Testimonies 65

Chapter 12: Your Prophetic History 67

Prophetic Principle: Bringing a Word of Correction ... 69

Chapter 13: Bread from Heaven 70

*Prophetic Principle: You Never Prophesy Complete
Revelation* 73

Chapter 14: Changing Names 75

Prophetic Principle: Speak Words Seasoned With Mercy 79

Chapter 15: Prophesying to Yourself 81

Prophetic Principle: Avoid the Invitation to Join the Fight 84

Chapter 16: Defining Moments 85

Prophetic Principle: Keep it Simple 88

Chapter 17: Right Direction, Wrong Altitude 90

Prophetic Principle: Seeing Through Prophetic Prisms 93

Chapter 18: When God Gets Our Attention 95

Prophetic Principle: Hijacked Meaning 99

Chapter 19: Changing Your Context 100

Prophetic Principle: When a Word is Not Received 102

Chapter 20: Honoring the Old Roads 104

Prophetic Principle: Incomplete Revelation 107

**Chapter 21: Finding Purpose in Shame and
    Humiliation** 109

Prophetic Principle: The Sounds of Silence 115

Chapter 22: The Challenge of Identity 118

Prophetic Principle: Reminders of a Forgotten History 121

Chapter 23: Divine Encounters I 122

Prophetic Principle: Speak Without Leaving a Bruise 126

Chapter 24: Divine Encounters II 128

Prophetic Principle: The Sound of Judgment-Free Prophecy .. 131

Chapter 25: Repurposed Lives 133

Prophetic Principle: Judgment and Consequence 135

Chapter 26: When Recognition Comes 137

Prophetic Principle: A Fast of Words 139

Chapter 27: Let God Make the Way 141

Prophetic Principle: The Boundary of Honor 143

Chapter 28: When Accusation Comes 145

Prophetic Principle: Standing in the Gap 148

Chapter 29: The Power of the Words You Speak 149

Prophetic Principle: Words of Hope in the Valley of Despair . 152

Chapter 30: Redefined Seasons 154

Prophetic Principle: Honoring Those Who Went Before 156

Chapter 31: You Become the Message You Carry 158

Prophetic Principle: Dissatisfied Seasons 161

Chapter 32: Speaking to an Angry and Frustrated Culture 162

Prophetic Principle: Prophesying Next Steps 164

Chapter 33: A Rediscovered History 166

Prophetic Principle: The Danger of Distance 170

Chapter 34: Delivering Hope 171

Prophetic Principle: When You Gain an Audience 174

Chapter 35: Prophetic Resolution 176

Prophetic Principle: When a Word Waits in Time 179

A FINAL WORD 181

But you should also desire the special abilities the Spirit gives—
especially the ability to prophesy.
—I Corinthians 14:1

FOREWORD

Learning to operate skillfully in the gift of prophecy can be difficult, especially given the independent nature of most prophetic people. In my 30+ years of prophetic ministry, I've learned countless, invaluable lessons and insights, but I came by much of it the hard way—on my own, through trial and error.

Armed with this powerful book, written by my friend Garris Elkins, you don't have to learn the hard way. Here is a simple-to-understand manual of profound insights forged in the fires of real-world experience. Garris' aim in writing *The Prophetic Voice* is to convey the essence of prophecy—what it is; how to understand it; how to give it; and most importantly, how to avoid the traps, fallacies and pitfalls common in exercising God's powerful gift to the prophetic community which is His Church.

This book gleams with nuggets, both practical and illuminating—simple things such as realizing that we are rarely given the complete revelation for a word. With this understanding alone, a host of ills can be avoided by those operating in prophecy who, though well-meaning, reach too deep into their personal wells for the missing words they are sure were omitted through their own shortcomings.

Garris' knowledge abounds throughout these pages. You will learn about God's timing in giving prophecy, how to discern between your thoughts and God's thoughts, how to accept the unknown nature of heavenly words destined for an earthly destination, how to relate to those you are prophesying to, and most importantly (in my opinion) when to speak and when to be silent.

While many think that the worst that can happen to a prophet is to be labeled "false," Garris illustrates the negative consequences of people coming to believe *too* much in your gift, either growing dependent on it or attempting to hijack it for their own means.

The key to everything Garris teaches in this systematic tome is that God knows what He's doing. It is up to us to allow Him to move as He sees fit. This becomes much less of a challenge when we are armed with the truth—the sage outlook of one who has been there, done it, and returned to share his wealth of knowledge with those on similar paths. God's words are simple, Garris tells us; it is we who complicate them.

Fortunately, there is nothing complicated about Garris' teaching. Whether you are a senior prophet or a nascent minister of God's Spirit, there is something here for you. After all, practice doesn't make perfect, it only makes permanent. Let this book flow through you as you glean the truths in the personal stories and testimonies resplendent on these pages.

I wish I had Garris' book 30 years ago. The path would have been much less arduous—for me and for those around me.

Dr. Harold R. Eberle
Founder of Worldcast Ministries
Yakima, WA

PREFACE

When Paul wrote to the church in Corinth, he expressed his desire that everyone be able to prophesy. That is also my desire and my purpose for writing this book.

There are excellent resources available with detailed instruction on how to prophesy. Entire schools exist to train people in prophecy. I would encourage you to take advantage of these resources and organizations. *The Prophetic Voice* is different. It is about the essence of prophecy. By essence, I mean the feel and function of the gift in the changing context of everyday life.

I define the gift of prophecy with a broad brushstroke: I believe everything God does on earth is prophetic. When the truth of Heaven invades the earth, something prophetic takes place. That is the nature of revelation. If we can enlarge our understanding of how God speaks, we can allow Him to uniquely speak through us without having to adopt another person's interpretation of the gift, its function, or a particular style of delivery.

This book is composed of chapters followed by prophetic principles. Each chapter and principle stand alone. The content of the chapter will rarely be reflected in the principle following it. This is by design and not intended to be confusing. My intent is to provide enough variable terrain in the book to keep you engaging the subject from different perspectives.

Many of the chapters contain personal stories illustrating my experience with the gift of prophecy. Your context and experience will be different. Despite our differences, the exercise of the gift of prophecy in our individual settings will share some things in common. That commonality is what I want you to see.

As you explore and develop this gift, enjoy the journey. God has so many good and hope-filled words He wants to speak through you to a world starving to know the loving and power-filled message of Heaven.

INTRODUCTION

God releases the gifts of His Spirit through encounters with Him. Scripture is filled with these encounters. Not all are dramatic, but they are encounters nonetheless. The first disciples had an experience with the Spirit that would start them on a journey to reach the world with the message of God's love. That encounter took place on the Day of Pentecost when a group of Spirit-indwelled believers would become Spirit-empowered believers in accordance with an instruction given earlier by the Lord:

> "But you will receive power when the Holy Spirit comes upon you. And you will be my witnesses, telling people about me everywhere—in Jerusalem, throughout Judea, in Samaria, and to the ends of the earth" (Acts 1:8).

The Church is a prophetic community whose voice was empowered on the Day of Pentecost to transmit the message of God's love to the people of earth. If we are going to understand how God uses His Church in the streets of our cities, we need to revisit the events of that day so we can understand His methods.

For the disciples who were living in fear of death after the crucifixion of Jesus, everything would change based on the events that took place in John 20. This huddled and confused group of disciples met the resurrected Jesus face to face when He appeared in their midst:

> *That Sunday evening the disciples were meeting behind locked doors because they were afraid of the Jewish leaders. Suddenly, Jesus was standing there among them! "Peace be with you," he said. As he spoke, he showed them the wounds in his hands and his side. They were filled with joy when they saw the Lord! Again he said, "Peace be with you. As the Father has sent me, so I am sending you." Then he breathed on them and said, "Receive the Holy Spirit"* (John 20: 19-22).

The reality of that one impartation had huge implications. In the Old Covenant, God's Spirit only visited people and then departed. In the New Covenant, the Spirit came and remained within each believer, transforming them into carriers of God's presence. A long-lost relationship with humanity was restored because of the events of John 20. Those assembled in the room that day became the first born-again people to walk on the face of the earth. Each of the first disciples was the *new person* Paul described in II Corinthians 5:17.

The promise of God walking with Adam and Eve in the cool of Eden's evening was returned with a single exhale of breath from the lungs of Jesus into His disciples. A creation event was taking place as Jesus breathed the Spirit into His followers. In that moment, God took His relationship with us to a higher level—higher even than the experience of Eden. We no longer wait to meet God for an evening walk. God now walks with us everywhere we go. We carry Him to the supermarket, to the mall, to a PTA meeting, and into buildings where the Church gathers. He is now the *everywhere, all the time God* who lives within us.

As carriers of God's Spirit, we were given possession of all the gifts and all the potential of His Spirit at the moment of our salvation—not dependent on our maturity or stature in life. This is the nature of God. He frontloads everything we need to live a Godly life. We spend the rest of our days unpacking the reality of what we already possess—including the astounding gifts of the Spirit and especially the gift of prophecy. If we underestimate the potential of what we carry, we can end up living lives that only rise to the limiting level of our underestimation. We will create theologies that confine our understanding of God and how He interacts with people to a small and powerless representation.

For the sake of this book, I want to simplify what I mean by prophecy. Anytime Heaven invades earth, something prophetic is taking place. Every time a word of knowledge or wisdom is released, we are encountering Jesus who is the Spirit of Prophecy. I want to remove the restraining and limiting definitions that have been assigned to prophecy. I want to remove blinders from our fields of vision and help us see more clearly the much larger work of God taking place in the world. God desires to speak through us to impact humanity by releasing Spirit-empowered words and actions of power and hope.

It was never God's intent that only a few would prophesy. The Apostle Paul said, *Let love be your highest goal! But you should also desire the special abilities the Spirit gives—especially the ability to prophesy* (I Corinthians 14:1). The word *especially* sticks out to me. Prophecy is an important gift God uses to transmit in word and image His heart for the world. We should all desire this gift.

I should pause here and distinguish between the gift of prophecy and the office of the prophet. Paul said we should all desire to prophesy. He made that statement knowing that not everyone is a prophet or holds the office of prophet simply because they gave a prophetic word. Moving forward in the gift of prophecy requires time, testing, and passing the integrity checks of the Spirit along the way; that is what can lead a person into the possible office of a prophet. The office of a prophet is one of the definitions found in Ephesians 4 that helps the Church grow into maturity. It is not an office we pursue but something we discover—something others will affirm as we grow in our relationship with Jesus and mature as a leader within His Church.

Paul said love should be our highest goal, but he also said we should desire—not neglect—the Spirit-empowered gifts. He had an entire list of gifts to choose, yet he said: desire *especially the ability to prophesy.* Paul placed a high regard on this gift. He wanted more than a select few to experience its beauty and power.

We have a tendency to overly define the spiritual gifts; we make lists of the gifts and their attributes—and we even test people for them. I'm not saying that's wrong, but it is simply too constraining when it comes to how the Spirit works in a person's life. God wants to expand our understanding of the gifts so that more of the Church will be willing to step up and begin to prophesy.

The Church has been positioned in every culture to speak with the empowered voice of Heaven. This is not only a message of the Good News for salvation; it is also a message of personal and cultural transformation.

When Peter and John were walking to the temple, as they had done many times before, it was a word of hope that released the physical healing for a crippled man and sent the city of Jerusalem into an uproar. Jerusalem was experiencing the beginning of a transformation because Peter told a man what God had revealed to him about his destiny. All transformation is the result of revelation. When Peter told the man to get up and walk in the name

8

of Jesus, those words contained the power to transform what appeared to be unchangeable.

The Church is silent when we do not understand that our voice is the vehicle God uses to release healing and transformation. He spoke a word to Peter and John, they shared that word with a crippled man, and a miracle took place. That is the essence and transformational power of prophecy.

Miracles are ready to be released into our world; they are lined up behind the Church, waiting for our voice to transmit their message of hope and healing. The miracles we read about in the Book of Acts were the result of someone hearing God's voice and speaking those words of healing as an act of obedience. Peter said to the crippled man, *Get up and walk!* Peter did not have to pray and request healing. He heard a word from the Holy Spirit, spoke it, and something wonderful took place.

I once had an encounter with Jesus in the middle of the night that radically changed my life forever—an encounter that would impact me and my family and every person I will ever meet throughout the course of my life. Each prophetic word I release will trace its origin back to that one event. I carry the essence of that encounter into each new day, expecting God to speak to others like He did to me.

As you read the stories arranged in the pages of this book, my hope is that you will have similar experiences with God. These God-encounters will forever change your life. God has plans to use your voice to transmit His hope to a hurting world.

CHAPTER 1
THE POWER OF ENCOUNTER

An encounter with God will change your life forever. I had such an encounter as a young man. Jesus became so real to me in the dark of night that to this day I am still touched by that experience.

In the 1970's, I was a law enforcement officer. I worked for a large sheriff's department in San Jose, California in the heart of the Silicon Valley—long before it was called by that name. In my youth, the valley was filled with orchards, but gradually the orchards gave way to housing tracts, freeways, and start-up tech businesses. It was in this valley as a young twenty-two-year-old that I raised my right hand to be sworn in as a sheriff's deputy.

After several years working as a deputy, I was ready to move. I was tired of the congestion and traffic. I needed more room and a new start. Jan and I decided to move to Oregon. And so, with our one-year-old daughter, Anna, we headed north to a new life, and I began a career with the police department in the city of Springfield.

Two years into working as a detective, my long-neglected faith began to stir within me. God's pursuit of me intensified. When our second child, David, was born,

Jan and I felt drawn back to church—something we had left behind during the first years of our marriage. We wanted to offer our children the same faith our parents had offered to us.

After a succession of disappointing visits to several local churches, we were encouraged by a friend to try a church in Eugene, Oregon, called Faith Center. When I walked in the door, I felt something was different. Those feelings were the beginning of a reconnection with God.

A hunger for God rose in my heart over the following weeks, though I was still living my life in a way that did not yet line up with that hunger.

We decided to have our two children dedicated to the Lord. The Sunday morning of the dedication would set in motion a series of events that would change my life forever.

Though I remember standing on the platform during the dedication, I cannot remember anything the pastor prayed. What I can tell you is that when hands were laid on me in prayer, something clicked. It felt as though God was turning the knob of a tumbler on the vault of my heart. When the final number to the combination of my locked and fearful heart clicked, I opened up to God. It wasn't dramatic, but I knew something had taken place beyond the dedication of our children. God was inviting me back to a destiny and calling I had run away from.

That night, as Jan and I lay in bed, we talked about the events of the day. I was still trying to figure it all out. As I lay in bed, a past commitment I had made to God in my childhood was being awakened. Jan went to sleep, and I was left alone with my thoughts.

At some point in the dark of that night, I sensed the presence of Jesus enter our bedroom. He walked over to my bedside and knelt down. I was frozen in place as this heavenly encounter took place. The Lord reached out and touched my chest, moving His hand from my throat down to my abdomen like He was unzipping me. As I lay bare before Him, the Lord took what looked like a large sponge from a basin filled with His blood and began to scrub out the dark recesses of my rebellious heart. This went on for what seemed like hours. I knew I was being forgiven for each commandment of God I had broken. When He was done, He moved His hand up my chest and "zipped" me back up.

A single syllable came from my mouth—a sound in a language I would later learn to be the language of Heaven, with a translation not found in earthly dictionaries. Then He left me to sleep the deep sleep of the forgiven.

The next morning, I did not hear Jan get up. I woke up much later than normal. When I walked into the kitchen, she turned to greet me and then tilted her head inquisitively to the side and asked, "What happened to you?" Knowing nothing of what I had experienced, Jan would later tell me my face looked completely different. I was manifesting on my countenance what had taken place in my spirit.

In response to Jan's question, I began to weep. I took her by the hand and we sat down on our couch where I began to confess every sin I had committed against her and God. I continued to weep as I repented. She too began to confess sin and repent of the condition of her own heart. We talked for hours. We were being set free. It was also the beginning of a real trust in our marriage, without which there can be no true love.

Jan would later tell her friends this was the only night she ever slept with two men. She went to bed with the old Garris and woke the next day to meet a new man.

The following morning, I drove from our home in Springfield into Eugene to the counseling offices of Faith Center. I needed to know what had happened to me. I needed someone to help me unpack the encounter I had with Jesus the night before. I shared my experience with one of the staff pastors, Morris Brown, and he responded by throwing his hands up in the air, laughing, and thanking God. Morris then began to patiently share with me what had taken place, showing me in Scripture where other believers had similar encounters with God.

For the next few weeks, I got emotional when I thought of God's goodness. This was a challenge for a police detective who needed to maintain a professional composure.

Everything in my life had changed. I couldn't get enough of my new church community. I was there every time the doors opened. I was hungry and on fire with God's love.

I started buying extra bags of groceries. In my unmarked detective vehicle, I would drive up to houses in the poorest neighborhoods in our city, walk quietly to the front door, set a bag of groceries on the front porch, and pound loudly on the door. I would run back to my car and watch the door open to see little children or struggling parents discover a waiting bag of food. I sat in my car and wept.

One of the first things to emerge from my encounter was the ability to hear and see what God was doing with new clarity. Today, we would describe what I was beginning to experience as the emergence of the gift of prophecy. I had no definition for what was taking place. I simply began to encourage and exhort people about the goodness of God. I also began to see spiritual realities that I had not previously discerned. That new sight began a journey I have walked in for the last forty years.

PROPHETIC PRINCIPLE
A PROMISED BREAKTHROUGH

The pressures of life are like a spiritual membrane that becomes stretched and distorted from its original design. In seasons of stress, we can become uncomfortable and unsure.

This stretching is part of the process of breakthrough. Just before things break open, it usually feels like you are trapped in an elastic-like resistance, keeping you just out of reach from the very promise you are pursuing. Don't run. Stay faithful. Once you break through the resistance, you will fall forward into the goodness of God.

Prophesy the breakthrough—not the difficulty—of the membrane experience. Everyone knows what it feels like to be stretched. Yet many of those same people do not know that a promise exists on the other side of each season of stretching.

Prophesy the higher reality of God's promise. Knowing a fulfilled promise will eventually be birthed is what gives people hope to keep pressing forward.

Chapter 2
A SUDDEN DEPOSIT

Suddenly, there was a sound from heaven like the
roaring of a mighty windstorm, and it filled the house
where they were sitting. — Acts 2:2

I will never forget the first time God spoke a word to me
and asked me to deliver it in a public gathering. This
happened just weeks after my encounter with Jesus in the
middle of the night. I was at Faith Center, a large church,
where several thousand people attended multiple services
each weekend. It was a sea of people.

The word came to me as an image during worship. I
saw a lighthouse on a rocky coastline with large waves
crashing and exploding against its immovable structure. It
was a dramatic image. I don't remember the full content of
the word, but it was a word of hope describing a "beacon
on a raging sea," assuring someone they would survive
navigating a challenging season of life because God was
their place of security.

I had no idea about prophetic protocol. I tugged on
the arm of an usher I had recently met and told him what I
was seeing. I watched the usher make his way forward

and speak to one of the pastors on the platform, while the church continued to worship. That pastor leaned over and shared something with another pastor who was leading the service.

Watching this interaction take place on the platform, I was not sure what would happen next. I couldn't imagine these pastors allowing a free-for-all in such a large gathering. Even at my immature level of exposure to public ministry, I was grateful for the protocol these leaders had wisely put in place. The pastor leading the service finished the song we were singing, and then he called on me. He asked me to share the word from where I was standing.

I had to shout in order to be heard. I was so afraid, that I closed my eyes as I spoke. The pastor repackaged my stumbling words into something people could actually understand and then applied the word, giving time for people to respond. It was all over in just a few moments, but it taught me something about how prophetic words come. A prophetic word often appears suddenly in our minds—without warning.

When the presence of God becomes tangible in word or deed, He breaks into the natural realm of chronological time, interrupting what is currently taking place around us. His revelation can be in stark contrast to our current circumstance, or it can bring a word of confirmation to what is taking place. Nothing is sudden or surprising in Heaven because it is a place filled with the constant and full revelation of God.

The words *sudden* or *suddenly* often define God's interaction with people in Scripture.

When God was delivering Israel from Egypt:

So Moses and Aaron did just as the LORD commanded them. As Pharaoh and all of his officials watched, Aaron raised his staff and struck the water of the Nile.

Suddenly, the whole river turned to blood! (Exodus 7: 20).

When Jericho was captured:

Suddenly, the walls of Jericho collapsed, and the Israelites charged straight into the town and captured it (Joshua 6:20).

When Elijah was caught up into Heaven:

As they were walking along and talking, suddenly a chariot of fire appeared, drawn by horses of fire. It drove between the two men, separating them, and Elijah was carried by a whirlwind into heaven (2 Kings 2:11).

When angels appeared to the shepherds announcing Jesus' birth:

That night there were shepherds staying in the fields nearby, guarding their flocks of sheep. Suddenly, an angel of the Lord appeared among them, and the radiance of the Lord's glory surrounded them (Luke 2:8-9).

When Jesus calmed the storm:

When Jesus woke up, he rebuked the wind and said to the waves, "Silence! Be still!" Suddenly the wind stopped, and there was a great calm (Mark 4:39).

When Jesus stood on the Mount of Transfiguration:

As the men watched, Jesus' appearance was transformed so that his face shone like the sun, and his clothes became as white as light. Suddenly, Moses and Elijah appeared and began talking with Jesus (Matthew 17:2-3).

When two disciples walked on the Road to Emmaus:

As they talked and discussed these things, Jesus himself suddenly came and began walking with them (Luke 24:15).

When the Spirit came on the Day of Pentecost:

Suddenly, there was a sound from heaven like the roaring of a mighty windstorm, and it filled the house where they were sitting (Acts 2:2).

When Jesus appeared to Paul on the Road to Damascus:

As he was approaching Damascus on this mission, a light from heaven suddenly shone down around him (Acts 9:3).

When Paul and Silas were set free from prison:

Suddenly, there was a massive earthquake, and the prison was shaken to its foundations. All the doors immediately flew open, and the chains of every prisoner fell off! (Acts 16:26).

The sudden nature of events throughout Scripture provides us with insight on how God intervenes in the course of human events. Identifying God's methods enhances our ability to understand how prophecy is received and delivered.

Prophecy can appear in the form of a word, dream, vision, impression, sound, or even a fragrance. It can be delivered through a spoken word, a painting, writing, preaching, acts of kindness—the ways are innumerable. While the reception and delivery of these prophetic words may not carry with them the dramatic element of a mighty rushing wind or a chariot of fire, our interaction with the Holy Spirit is still both empowering and effective.

To this day, after delivering hundreds of prophetic words, I am still delighted and surprised when they suddenly appear. My delight comes because what I am hearing or seeing was just a moment ago in Heaven waiting for delivery on earth. Each time a word comes, I am surprised—not a surprise that comes from disbelief but a surprise like a child would experience on Christmas morning when they are about to unwrap a wonderful gift delivered by a loving Father.

PROPHETIC PRINCIPLE
THE VOICE OF HUMILITY

Over the years of serving the Lord in various forms of prophetic ministry, I have noticed something. The most life-impacting words come when spoken from a heart of humility. Humility works as a spiritual filter, straining out the grit of our human pride that so easily rears its head and plugs the flow of our effectiveness.

Pride is fueled when we allow a delusional image of our importance to run rampant in our mind. The result of this unbridled pride can produce hurtful—even brutal—words spoken in God's name. The most powerful prophetic voices I know sound more like a merciful father running out to welcome home a prodigal child. This is a voice that invites a son to a celebration in his honor, reminding him of his true identity and inheritance.

Chapter 3
DELAYED DELIVERY

A man I know, who has significant influence and is respected all around the world, had taken the primary leadership role in a large, international organization. It was assumed that he would remain in that position for many years to come.

One morning as I was praying, this man came to mind, and I heard the Lord say, "He will bring a surprise." I was not sure what that meant. I asked the Lord and He said, "He will withdraw himself." When I heard those words, I had a sense of what they might mean, but I didn't have a sense of what to do with them.

I sat on the word and waited for the Lord to tell me what to do. A few days later, the Lord asked me to contact the man. The content of a word and the timing of its delivery are two separate things. Each prophetic word will contain these two elements.

I called the leader and shared with him the word about the *surprise*. There was silence on the other end of the phone line after I spoke. He broke the silence by asking, "Was there anything more to the word?" When I replied there was nothing more, we continued to talk for a few minutes more and then ended the call.

Shortly after the phone call, I heard an announcement that this man would be stepping down from his current role of leadership. The news was described as a "surprise" to all involved. The word I delivered confirmed something already taking place in the man's heart.

I share this story because there is something I want you to see. It has to do with waiting—sitting on a word that does not have a delivery date yet attached. We can assume that just because we hear a prophetic word we are required to immediately share it. This is not always true. The delivery of a word can be very strategic, and its greatest impact comes when it is delivered in God's timing.

I could have impatiently stepped over the process and delivered the word out of synch with God's original intent and timing, but I might have interfered with something important that was taking place behind the scenes. Unseen elements are always at work. These elements may not be part of the original message and need time to develop.

God always wants to partner with us and arrange circumstances to make a word ready to be received. If a word is given too early, it can lack the impact that would have come once all the supporting elements were in place. When I was asked if there was anything more to the word, I had personal opinions on the subject, but they were not part of the original word the Lord asked me to share.

As God increases your sensitivity and ability to speak in His name, ask Him to give you an understanding of His timing. God wants to use you in unusual ways to influence and encourage others.

Waiting for His timing before you speak is part of your prophetic training.

But the Holy Spirit produces this kind of fruit in our lives: love, joy, peace, patience, kindness, goodness, faithfulness, gentleness, and self-control (Galatians 5:22-23).

PROPHETIC PRINCIPLE
DEALING WITH PUSHBACK

I write every day. Some things I write are on-going projects that could someday become a book or an article. Some of what I write will never be seen.

God has opened doors for me to occasionally connect with people I would never know had it not been for some publication on social media or in a book. This can also create awkward and unfamiliar responses.

Recently, I got some pushback for something I wrote. This happens from time to time. The pushback came from a person I do not know who felt that everything written has to be backed up with Scripture. He wanted a chapter and verse for everything.

When it comes to writing or speaking words of prophecy, not everything we write or say needs a chapter and verse to be from God. Yes, the essence of what we communicate should align with Scripture, but even the people we read about in Scripture did not constantly quote Bible verses back and forth to each other in their daily conversations. The Bible as we know it was not available in their lifetime.

If you are going to speak or write as a representative

of Jesus Christ, make sure you know His heart as well as you know His word. There will be times when you won't have a Scripture verse to back up what you say, but you will know what you are saying is accurately reflecting God's heart. It was God's heart that motivated Him to write His word. That order of revelation is important to remember when we speak in His name.

Chapter 4
REVEALING HIDDEN THINGS

There are times when a word will come to you out of left field. A friend of ours, Ella (not her real name), had taken a staff position in a large church. The ministry of the church and its senior pastor appeared to be very successful. Ella is gifted in writing and was used by the pastor as an in-house editor for his writing projects.

Ella came to visit us for a few days. We always enjoyed our time together. Good friends feed your soul. One evening during our visit, Jan and I took time to pray over Ella. We don't assume we will always have a word to share. We begin in prayer. If God has something He wants to speak, we will be faithful to deliver it.

An image began to emerge before my eyes as we prayed. I saw the pastor of Ella's church wearing a long, robe-like garment. In the picture, the pastor's robe was opened, revealing hidden flowerpots on the ground at his feet. There were no beautiful flowers in the pots. Instead, the pots were filled with plants, and each plant was marked with the word "deception." Unless the robe was pulled back, the pots would never have been seen.

These kinds of prophetic images can be very hard to

deliver. But more important than hurting someone's feelings or sounding negative is our desire to be faithful and obedient to the word of the Lord. Ella, Jan, and I had ministered together in numerous settings. We each knew the value of honor. We desired to live in peace with all people as far as possible. Giving such a word carried with it a certain level of trust.

When I shared the word of warning, none of us knew what to make of it. Warnings are not comfortable. If what I saw was accurate, there would be personal ramifications for the pastor and for Ella because she worked for him. We prayed for the pastor, wanting to cover him and extend grace if he was in trouble.

Several months after that visit, we got word of sad events taking place in the church where Ella worked. A deceitful relationship in the pastor's life emerged, resulting in separation and divorce. The church was deeply affected and filled with great sorrow at what was taking place. As the situation continued to unfold, other areas of deception began to emerge that had previously been hidden in the life of this pastor.

How did I know what would happen? I didn't. The word did not fit what I knew in the natural. I knew nothing until the Lord revealed the image to me of the robe and the pots. I was only asked to transmit a warning from God. Warnings have tremendous value. They are meant to prepare us and protect us and provide a place of safety in difficult times.

You will have times when a word may not fit the context you see playing out in the natural. Go with the nudge of the Spirit. This is how we learn to discern and deliver a word from the Lord.

God would surely have known it, for he knows the secrets of every heart (Psalm 44: 21).

PROPHETIC PRINCIPLE
WHEN TO REMAIN SILENT

The prophetic gift is not a water faucet you turn on and off at your pleasure. There will be times when you do not have a word to share. It is important for your integrity and for the safety of those to whom you minister that you do not put yourself in a place where you always have to produce a word from the Lord. A danger lurks when you feel compelled to prophesy out of human imagination. The fear of not having something to say can trigger your pride. You may feel like you always need to speak in order to validate your gift. This unhealthy need to be heard can lead you to a place of compromise.

Waiting until the Lord speaks can be a challenge when you have someone standing before you in desperate need of hope. Hope can be delivered in different ways, not just through prophetic ministry. When you don't hear a word from God, you can still speak words of destiny, blessing, and hope that apply to all believers. The Scripture is filled with these words. Learn them: they are powerful.

When you begin to minister to someone and you do not immediately have something to share, pray and ask the Lord what He wants you to do. Jesus only did what He saw the Father doing. Jesus is our model in all aspects of life.

As you learn when to speak and when to remain silent, you will develop a deeper acuity for the Spirit's voice that only comes with discernment, not assumption.

Be still in the presence of the LORD and wait patiently for him to act (Psalm 37:7).

CHAPTER 5
INQUIRE OF THE LORD

When Jan and I were based in Berlin, Germany, our assignment had us traveling quite a lot. Most weeks we found ourselves on an airplane or in a train en route to a different European nation. On these trips, we met wonderful people in many diverse cultural settings.

On one such trip, I had finished teaching, and the meeting was coming to a close. A young man walked up to me. In a nervous voice, he said, "I think I have a word for you." He went on to share that giving prophetic words was something new and strange to him, but he wanted to be obedient. He told me the story of the Gibeonite deception found in the book of Joshua. His word was to remind me that I should always inquire of the Lord. After the meeting, I went to the Scripture to review the incident surrounding the deception.

Joshua 9 tells the story of the Gibeonites. They heard how Joshua and Israel had defeated Jericho and Ai, and they did not want to be next in line for a devastating defeat. They set up a ruse to get the Israelites to believe they had come from a distant land and were not from the nearby nations Israel was planning to engage in battle.

But when the people of Gibeon heard what Joshua had done to Jericho and Ai, they resorted to deception to save themselves. They sent ambassadors to Joshua, loading their donkeys with weathered saddlebags and old, patched wineskins. They put on worn out, patched sandals and ragged clothes. And the bread they took with them was dry and moldy. When they arrived at the camp of Israel at Gilgal, they told Joshua and the men of Israel, "We have come from a distant land to ask you to make a peace treaty with us" (Joshua 9:3-6).

After hearing the Gibeonite's story, Israel made a terrible mistake:

So the Israelites examined their food, but they did not consult the LORD. Then Joshua made a peace treaty with them and guaranteed their safety, and the leaders of the community ratified their agreement with a binding oath (Joshua 9:14-15).

Israel looked at the natural evidence the Gibeonites presented, but they did not inquire of the Lord. As a result, they bound themselves to an agreement that would forever require Israel to come to the defense of the Gibeonites, who were supposed to be one of the conquered nations as Israel took possession of the Promised Land. The Gibeonites and Israel's agreement with them would become a visible scar on the nation of Israel and the leadership of Joshua.

One of the challenges you will face in communicating a word from God is your attempt to evaluate a situation based only on the available physical evidence. Asking the Lord to reveal the truth that exists behind what you are seeing with your natural sight will keep you from being easily deceived.

Jan and I took this warning seriously. Warnings are precious gifts. Although we were in the habit of inquiring and not just assuming, the fact that God chose to specifically remind us held a stronger incentive to be on the alert.

The word from the young man was a gift for more than just that current season. Unknown to us, we were entering a time where we would make significant life decisions and enter a larger transition than we first thought. At every turn, we would inquire of the Lord and then experience His amazing grace. The passage in Joshua became a reminder of God's promise and provision. We might get shaken, but because we inquired of the Lord at every turn, we had confidence in His protection and peace. We will always be grateful for that word the young man had the courage to deliver.

I also loved the fact that God spoke to us through someone who was new to the gift of prophecy. He was nervous and maybe a bit fearful, but he was obedient. His obedience had a significant impact on our lives.

I want to encourage all of you who are just beginning your prophetic journey. Listen and speak what the Lord gives you. Humbly submit the word and trust God to use it for His glory. The impact of your voice is not determined by your chronological age or your current level of experience. The impact of a word is empowered by the Spirit of God.

God wants us to inquire of Him before we speak for Him. Our ministry is not to always prophesy what is obvious. We often speak of what is not yet seen. God has called us to look with the eyes of the Spirit into the situations of life and see what only He can make known.

Like the prophet Elijah, we will discover that the word of God is not always in the wind, fire, and earthquake, but often in the still, small voice of God. God's voice has the

power to protect us from impatient decisions.
Always remember to inquire of the Lord.

PROPHETIC PRINCIPLE
PROPHESYING INTO DARK PLACES

One morning, as I sat at my chair in the predawn darkness, a goose flew overhead and honked. I wondered how the goose could navigate through the darkness, and then I remembered something from my past. In my days as a pilot, I made early morning departures from an airport deep in a mountain valley, often wrapped in the predawn hours of darkness. After takeoff, I would climb up to my cruising altitude and be able see what I could not see from the runway in the valley. My flight path had taken me to a higher altitude where I entered the first rays of a new sunrise not yet visible from the valley below.

On Easter morning, Mary, Peter, and John came to the empty tomb while it was still dark. The evidence of the resurrection was first revealed in the lingering darkness of that early morning. Heaven's message of hope was orchestrated in the brilliant altitude of God's glory and then poured out into the dark place of Jesus' crucifixion.

The darkness you see in the world around you is not a barrier to the revelation of God. Resurrection always targets places still wrapped in darkness. It is in the darkness where the first rays of hope will be seen and heard. When you speak a prophetic word of hope, it will carry with it the power of the first resurrection and the dawn of something new.

Chapter 6
PROPHETIC ALIGNMENT

Alignment is one of the most powerful results of a prophetic word. A word has the potential to align us with our God-designed destiny and calling. A business can be aligned with a product and an unrealized market. A ministry can be realigned to its abandoned purpose. Alignment can turn us in a completely new direction, or it can realign us with God's original intent for our lives. Alignment adjusts the course of our lives so we are able to move in the direction of the Spirit's leading.

Recently, I needed to get the wheels on my car aligned. I set up an appointment with one of our local tire dealerships. After examining my car, the mechanic discovered that I needed new shocks and struts. I also needed new tires.

Tires can reveal obvious signs of wear, but sometimes the real problem is unseen. In my case, the worn shocks and struts no longer provided the proper support for the wheels. The mechanic said the reason my tires were wearing down unevenly was because shocks and struts will lose strength over time, and the tire will begin to bounce up and down on the pavement. This bouncing will cause the tire to lose the full potential of its traction and will shorten the tread life by thousands of miles.

The same principle applies to the people to whom you deliver a prophetic word. There is more going on than just the signs of obvious wear. Most people begin to show signs of emotional and spiritual wear when they have traveled for a season out of alignment with God and His purpose for their lives. They can look spiritual and say all kinds of right-sounding things, but because they are not in line with God's will, they begin to show signs of premature wear. The wear can be revealed in a loss of hope, a negative response to life, or a separation from relationships. A prophetic word has the ability to reach into a heart and point out what is causing the real problem.

Over the years, I have come to realize that when I am tired and worn, I don't always recognize what I am dealing with. In these times, the way forward is a word of hope. In fact, I believe the way forward always contains a word of hope. Not only can hope lead us, but it also gives us the ability to believe another chance is available. At that point of realization, we can begin to realign our thoughts and actions with the promise of a hope-filled future.

When my mechanic revealed the problem, it actually felt good to find out the real reason for my worn tires. If I had left the dealership that day with new tires only—not knowing the real cause for the wearing—it would have been an expensive and short-term solution. I needed to know the deeper issue that was actually causing the wear. Such is the nature of prophetic ministry.

Prophetic Principle
RESIST THE URGE

Where the freedom of the Spirit is welcome, I have always sensed an urge to prophesy. I have been in meetings where multiple words came to me, and I knew they would apply to what was taking place. Many of these urges come simply because I am familiar with the prophetic gift, but most of the time they are not words to share publicly. They are points of revelation on how to pray and see the will of the Father accomplished.

The Apostle Paul gave wise instruction about public meetings. The public meetings of his day were home groups. The large gatherings we have today were later developments in Church history.

In I Corinthians 14, Paul called for local leadership to function at times like a spiritual traffic cop. He said, *No more than two or three should speak in tongues* (v. 27) and *Let two or three people prophesy* (v. 29). Paul even gives permission to interrupt a word of prophecy: *but if someone is prophesying and another person receives a revelation from the Lord, the one who is speaking must stop* (v. 30).

When was the last time you heard of a prophecy in progress that was interrupted? Not everyone who thinks they have a word from God should speak in a meeting. If everyone did as they wished, we would have no room left in our gatherings for anything else.

As you mature in your prophetic gift, you will come to realize that God doesn't need you to speak in order for His truth to be communicated. Others in the room are also able to communicate the heart of God.

Paul's directives can offend those who fail to realize the multi-faced purpose of a public gathering. He said, *Remember that people who prophesy are in control of their spirit and can take turns* (I Corinthians 14:32).

CHAPTER 7
WORDS THAT REDEFINE

When I was pastoring my second church, I experienced a major transition. After nine years in the ministry, I began to feel spiritually restless, and I did not understand why. The restlessness was not a negative; it was a Spirit-led notice that comes when God is getting ready to bring change. He must first make us willing to disengage from our current assignment so that we can engage something new. But if we are in a place we enjoy and love, it can be confusing. The restlessness can seem out of place and uninvited. There have been times I have rebuked this feeling, thinking it wasn't from God.

In the midst of my restlessness that year, our international church family held their annual convention at the Ridgecrest Conference Center in North Carolina. My spiritual father in the faith and friend, Roy Hicks Jr., and I flew his small plane from Oregon across the United States to attend the conference. We had fun getting to the conference, and we took several days to complete the journey.

When we landed in North Carolina, Roy had some meetings to attend, so I had time to explore the countryside. I drove through the beautiful back roads of North Carolina, thinking and processing what was next in my life. I had been restless for some time. My thoughts became questioning prayers about what God was trying to say to me. I wanted to get past the restless feelings to a place of answers.

One evening before a general session was to start, I sat on the front steps of the main auditorium. I was deep in thought when a man I knew by name only came up and sat by me. His name was Glen Pummel. I knew who Glen was from the information I received in the mail about our missionary personnel. Glen and his wife were missionaries to Chile. They had mentored a national church movement in that nation for many years. He was known as a proven and trusted leader.

After our initial exchange of greetings, Glen could tell I was processing some things in my life. I shared with him the strange and uninvited feelings I was having. He began to ask me a few questions. I answered that I was sensing a change in assignment and location. I told him I felt God was saying something to me about missions work. I also shared that I was feeling a disconnection as a pastor. It was a strange feeling because I really loved the city where we lived, the church, and the people we served.

As I talked with Glen about what was taking place in my life, I remembered a humorous story about obtaining my passport. I told the story to Glen.

Months earlier I heard the Lord say, "Get a passport." I really didn't care to travel. A few weeks later the Lord turned up the intensity of His request and said again, "Get a passport!"

When I heard this request for a second time, I put out a fleece. I asked the Lord to confirm His desire for me to get a passport. I would share the story at our next church council meeting. If the council mentioned they would be willing to pay for it, I would obey. I am so glad God is a patient Father, who has a heart of mercy toward us when we drag our feet.

The night of our council meeting, after we completed our regular business, I shared the story about God asking me to get a passport. Instead of asking any questions, the council all laughed and said, "We'll pay for it!" I had forgotten that the previous two pastors of the church ended up being sent overseas as missionaries. These wise leaders could see a familiar pattern developing. They were beginning to see one of the callings of that church was to release pastors into overseas missions work.

A few days later, I submitted my application for a passport. By the time of my trip to North Carolina, I had the passport in my possession, but no place to travel—yet. God was assembling all the pieces needed to make the transition while I was still trying to figure out the bigger picture.

With well-crafted words of wisdom, Glen told me the restlessness I was feeling was because God was shifting the mantle of my calling. I was trying to process my future from a pastor's point of view, and it was not working. Glen provided me with a fresh perspective and a first look at a new assignment.

He said, "The reason you are feeling this way is because God is shifting you from pastoral ministry to apostolic ministry." When Glen said those words, suddenly the restlessness lifted and clarity came. I had no details for any assignment or a future location, but Glen's words helped me see my future in a different context.

The conversation on the conference center steps was brief, but it had long-term effects on my life. Within months, Jan and I would pack and move from Newport, Oregon to Los Angeles, California. We would take a position in the missions department of our denomination. That first step led us to two deployments in the years that followed. We found ourselves sent to the West Indies and

Europe. In nine years, I traveled to thirty countries. Each of those assignments linked back to a man able to see a pastor in the middle of a personal struggle and willing to provide a simple word of definition that would bring the clarity needed to take the next step.

You will also encounter times like this. You will start out not knowing what to say, but during the course of a conversation, the Lord will give you a word of definition. That word will bring the same kind of clarity I received many years ago. The prophetic word you deliver will become a life-defining word for that person.

When God spoke creation into being He said, *Let there be light* (Genesis 1:3). He would use that same phrase, *Let there be*, as He continued to define the elements of the world He was about to create. Each element of the created world came into being through these same defining proclamations.

Definition will always precede creation. God gave new names to people in Scripture before He created a new life for them around the assignment attached to their new name. Think of Abram, Jacob, Simon, and others. Each name change carried a new assignment.

As you prophesy, you will be speaking words that affirm God's love and care for people. At times you will bring a word of definition. These words will help people see their lives from Heaven's perspective. Never be shy about releasing these words. You are not telling someone how to live. You are simply bringing a word of definition. In turn, that person will begin to see clearly enough to make their own decisions.

I am grateful for that word of definition on the steps of the conference center. In the following years, God would deliver His direction for my life through the voices of other faithful people, bringing the confirmation I would need to take the next step. What began with a feeling of restlessness ended with a deeper sense of trust in God's faithfulness to help me find my way forward when no way was visible.

Prophetic Principle
Don't Take It Personally

At some point, you will share a word with someone and they will not like what they hear. They may disagree with the content or delivery of your word.

These challenges can happen easily and rapidly in the immediate world of social media.

Some people will take the liberty of judging your life and the content of your theology based on a single paragraph of insight you share. Take comfort: the same thing happened in the Early Church when some people complained that Paul's letters were too forceful.

Be careful when you deal with any negative response. These interactions carry the potential of offense. If you are a rational, feeling, human being, you will have a reaction. Give your reaction to God—immediately. A wasted moment of offense will begin a work in your heart that can actually hijack your voice for the purpose of another kingdom. Forgive your critics and move on. God never promised everyone would agree with everything you say or write.

CHAPTER 8
DECLARING THE MYSTERIES OF HEAVEN

As a nineteen-year-old in the middle of the Jesus Movement, I was like so many other young people of that era: we were all searching for something.

The summer of 1969 was an unusual time in the culture of the United States. Everything was changing. God was reaching out and touching thousands of young men and women, and I was one of them.

I was living in the San Francisco Bay Area at the time. I couldn't get enough of the Bible and fellowship. I attended Bible studies in coffee houses and church services at places like the Peninsula Bible Church. I sat with hundreds of other young people in standing-room only crowds listening to Ray Stedman preach. One of these journeys took me to Bethany Bible College in Scotts Valley, California. Bethany was hosting a conference open to the public. A friend and I got into my VW bug and made the drive to Scotts Valley from my home in Los Gatos.

When we stepped into the auditorium, it was packed wall to wall. Young people with long hair and sandals stood around the perimeter of the main seating area. We found an available place to stand in the very back of the auditorium.

I grew up in a very conservative church. I had never experienced the Holy Spirit moving during worship in the ways I was seeing. It was strange and uncomfortable, but it was also right and good. Despite the strangeness, nothing was out of order. For the first time in my life, I felt the manifest presence of God being welcomed in a public gathering. I was drawn to this new and unfamiliar work of the Spirit.

The people conducting the service sat in rows of chairs on the platform. I don't recall who they were, but they looked important to my nineteen-year-old self.

About halfway through worship, one of the men sitting on the platform raised his head and looked out past the platform lighting and across the audience. I watched him as he scanned the crowd. He stopped and looked in our direction. I thought nothing of it, thinking he could be looking at a hundred other people who were standing along the back wall.

I watched as the man stood from his chair and walked through the worship team and down onto the main floor. He began walking in my direction. It was still impossible to think he was walking toward me, but he continued in my direction until it became more and more obvious that he was. When he was about ten feet away, he locked eyes with mine as he closed the remaining steps between us.

The man looked to be in his late seventies. He was wearing a suit and tie and carried a blend of authority and gentleness. He came and stood directly in front of me. Then he did something that made me really uncomfortable. He put his arms on my shoulders and pulled me close. He began to speak into my ear in a language I had never heard before. I would later come to know this heavenly language of the Spirit in a very personal way. On that day, the foreign language the man spoke into my ear was as strange as the meeting that was taking place.

The man only spoke briefly. He then pulled away and looked into my eyes for another second, turned, and made his way back to the front. I knew something holy had just taken place, but I was not sure what it was. At the close of the meeting later that evening, I drove back to my parent's home in Los Gatos still pondering what had taken place.

I parked that experience in the back of my mind and forgot about it. Ten years later, Jesus would visit me in the middle of the night, supernaturally transforming my life forever. Within weeks of that visit, the Lord took me back to that time when I was nineteen and attending the conference at Bethany. The Lord said, "I am bringing the interpretation of the words the man spoke into your ear. Your life will be a living interpretation of what was spoken to you that day by my Spirit."

These experiences are mysterious. We can forget we are interacting with the God of Heaven who spoke galaxies into existence by just a word. Much of what God does remains in the realm of mystery until we find ourselves living out a new reality we never imagined was possible.

When the elderly man made his way toward me, he did not have the full picture of what would take place in my life. He was simply responding to the Spirit. When he prayed by the unction of the Holy Spirit in his spiritual language, he did not know what he was saying. He did not give me the interpretation. Like the Apostle Paul said in I Corinthians 14:14: *For if I pray in tongues, my spirit is praying, but I don't understand what I am saying*. Like Paul, the man who prayed into my ear only knew he was praying a message from the Holy Spirit.

You will need to become comfortable with the mysterious part of prophetic ministry. Much of prophecy is straightforward and simple to understand, but it will carry a dimension of mystery you want to leave alone and not try to explain. God is the only one who can accurately unpack the mysteries of Heaven.

Remain open to the nudges of the Spirit. Like the elderly gentleman, you will sometimes go to a person being highlighted—maybe someone you have never met before. Speak what the Spirit gives you, and trust Him with the outcome. As you release the mysterious and wonderful words of the Spirit, they will help direct the course of someone in ways you never could have imagined.

Prophetic Principle
PROPHESYING HOPE TO THE NEXT GENERATION

Each generation will receive prophetic words from fathers and mothers of the faith. Jan and I have had these kinds of words spoken over us. When we experienced hard times, we revisited those words to stay on course. In the process, we refocused our thinking and reset our steps.

When Jan and I began pastoring almost four decades ago, we were walking into an uncharted landscape. There were times when we wanted to give up and times when we missed the mark. Along the way, we discovered that two things were always waiting for us. We discovered God was always present in our future, waiting for us to arrive. And when we arrived, we experienced the fulfillment of some of the words spoken over us in years gone by.

This encouragement became our invitation to taste and see the goodness of God for each new adventure of faith. Words of hope have no expiration date. They reside in our future, waiting to be grasped with believing hearts and lived out with anticipation.

CHAPTER 9
CHANGING HISTORY

One day, while Jan and I lived in Europe, something unusual happened. I was going about my daily routine when the Holy Spirit put a concern on my heart—a sense of urgency to pray over a developing situation. A picture formed in my mind; I saw a younger woman taking advantage of an elderly man. A critical hour was approaching and, if not stopped, a form of elder abuse would occur. The image became even more significant when I recognized the older man: Tim, the brother of June (not their real names). June was an elderly woman who I had pastored some years earlier, back in the United States.

As the image continued to unfold in my mind, I heard instructions from the Lord on how to pray. I was to bind an effort by the young woman to take the man's money through an act of deception that would also rob Tim's widowed sister of the financial help he had promised to her in her remaining years.

I declared: "In the Name of Jesus Christ, I command all abuse to be stopped. I break the influence and manipulation of this woman. I declare an end to this abuse. Tim, wake up and come to your senses. I speak deliverance and safety over you."

I spoke these prayers from my home in Berlin, Germany, to stop an ungodly transaction that was about to take place thousands of miles away in the United States. After I prayed, I went on with life.

Not long after I prayed that prayer, Jan and I were in Croatia when I received a phone call to contact June. Some years before, she had asked me if I could help her with the burial of her brother when he passed. She was not able to travel or handle these details alone. Now she was contacting me to let me know Tim had died, and she was left with the overwhelming task of making all the final arrangements for the disposal of her brother's estate.

June had been widowed for many years. She relied on her meager Social Security income and occasional financial support from her brother, Tim, when unexpected bills appeared. His help over the years had saved her from tremendous financial difficulty. Thankfully, we had already made plans to be in the States within a matter of days and we were grateful for God's timing. We wanted to honor this dear woman and keep our commitment to help her. A few days earlier than planned, we left Croatia and drove to Frankfurt, Germany, where we boarded a flight back to the United States.

We picked June up and drove her many miles out of state to her brother's home. Upon our arrival, we heard a sad story. Tim had become depressed upon the death of his wife several years earlier. His one outing and social contact was to visit a local café each morning for breakfast. Working at the restaurant was a waitress who started showing Tim special attention. Over several years, she had talked this vulnerable and lonely old man out of thousands of dollars and a vehicle. She was in the final stages of having him sign over his entire estate to her, including his home. Just days before the documents were to be signed— making the waitress the sole heir to his estate—Tim died.

These events had been just beginning when the Lord asked me to pray, thousands of miles away. Later, I asked the Lord why all of this had transpired, and He said, "I called Tim home before he would do something that would harm his legacy and put his sister in a place of jeopardy."

In the final days before his death, Tim refused to let the waitress into his home. The neighbors reported that she would knock on the door and windows and call out, but Tim would yell back that she needed to leave. On the day Tim stopped answering her from inside the house, the waitress grew concerned. She called the police. When they entered his home, they found him deceased. His body was removed, and the house was sealed. Thinking the legal transaction of a new will was complete, the waitress contacted June to let her know her brother had passed away. That set in motion the call to me in Europe.

We took June to the local bank and met with the banker who handled Tim's financial affairs. After June produced a death certificate and proper identification, the banker was able to share further details about what had been set in motion but which Tim's death had stopped. He showed us the legal paper trail of the proposed transfer of property, awaiting a new will that was never completed. In just days, Tim's estate would have been signed over to the waitress, leaving June without a penny. By the intervening mercy of God, Tim's legacy would not be darkened by this event, and his sister could now live out her remaining years in financial security.

When we entered Tim's home, it exhibited a life closed off from reality. Piles of random, handwritten notes were stacked atop the tables. The house was not dirty but cluttered—the result of Tim having been too ill and elderly to properly care for his home. His neighbors rarely saw him. He had become isolated and reclusive. The daily trip to the café became his major life event, and it also became a place where he was easy prey for an unscrupulous person.

June put Tim's home in the hands of a realtor who would auction the household items and prepare the property for sale. Just before doing so, June and her family cleaned the home and discovered a hidden treasure. Tim had hidden several bags of silver and gold coins and small gold bars in the house: an added blessing. Within a month, the house was sold and the bank accounts transferred into June's name.

June lived for another decade in the promise and provision of the Lord. She carried the memory of God's awesome intervention when He had provided for her in such a special way. Upon her death, June was able to pass on a financial heritage to her children and grandchildren. I got to partner with God in declaring a prayer that helped abort an evil plan. I also got to see a dear woman experience a season of peace and plenty in her later years. That was the best blessing of all.

You will never fully know the results of your prayers and prophetic declarations at the time you release them. You may never know the results this side of eternity. Like the situation with June and Tim, there will be times when God will demonstrate the power of prayers and declarations in dramatic fashion. He gives us a glimpse into something supernatural that fuels our future obedience. He also reminds us that when He asks us to do something, things will be set in motion that are beyond what we could ever dare to ask or think.

PROPHETIC PRINCIPLE
WHEN YOU SAID TOO MUCH

There will come a time when you realize you said too much and went beyond the scope of the simple word God gave you to share. These times are great opportunities to discover the depth of your integrity.

Integrity is important in all aspects of life. Once you lose your integrity, regaining it can be a challenge. We all make mistakes. Sharing a word from God is not done with perfection because God uses fallible people to transmit His message. God knows about our weakness and our propensity to want to appear error free. If we find ourselves contemplating how to sustain the pride-induced delusion of prophetic perfection, the only way out of that predicament is through personal disclosure and the admitting of our mistake.

You may fear losing credibility, but just the opposite is true. Letting a known mistake go uncorrected is where the real damage is done. Disclosure actually restores credibility.

Make a decision early on to challenge your own mistakes. If you shared a word with an individual or group that went beyond the scope of what God wanted you to share, admit it. You might say to yourself, "Who would know? Why not just let the word remain?" The Lord will know. He is the ultimate audience for the words you speak.

Once you realize your mistake and correct it, most people will honor your transparency and trust will deepen. Even more important, God will be able to trust you with His message. Honesty and humility are refreshing and rare. Speak your words of self-disclosure and move on. You simply navigated an integrity check that everyone must pass through as they learn to speak for God. If God can trust you with His message, more revelation will come. The continuation of these revelations will require us to possess a humble heart of integrity.

Chapter 10
NAVIGATING CORRECTION

When I was a younger pastor I tried different ways to teach and lead. During my early training and learning period, it was popular for pastors to use an abundance of sermon illustrations. Pastors created immense files of illustrations catalogued by topic. One pastor I knew had a file with over 10,000 sermon illustrations. He had each of them linked in his computer to various subjects. He would type in a topic and up would come a selection of illustrations to fit his sermon.

I got caught up in the sermon illustration frenzy. I spent hours each week searching for new illustrations and logging them under a reference system. If I had a three-point sermon, I would have an illustration for the introduction, an illustration for each sermon point, and one for the conclusion. If you enjoyed hearing stories and illustrations, you would have enjoyed what I was teaching. But this model of preaching had a problem.

About six months into this new style of preaching, a woman in our church approached me after the service. She said, "I am leaving the church." I asked her if she would tell me why. She said, "Lately, when I come to church, I can't get through all the stories and illustrations to actually hear the Word. I want the Word, not the stories."

When Jan and I returned home that day, I shared the conversation with her. I assumed she would come to my defense. Jan said, "She is right." I was floored. I value Jan's wisdom the most. More than anything, I wanted to preach the Word, but I had slipped into a blind spot that God had lovingly exposed. The woman's correction and my wife's agreement with her assessment became a wake up call for me.

I asked the Lord what I should do. He gave me some detailed instruction. He said to get rid of my illustration file and only keep the illustrations that had a direct connection to my life. He went on to tell me I was to live each week aware of my surroundings and what was taking place in the larger culture. He would provide all the illustrations I would ever need for my weekly sermon preparation from those two sources.

I made those corrections many years ago and have never looked back. I also never came up short when I needed an occasional illustration to enhance and illustrate part of a message. There is nothing wrong with a story or two, but in the end, I learned how to send people away with the Word, not with stories and illustrations.

Before I entered the ministry, I remember my pastor saying, "Any little old lady who knows her Bible can correct any prophet, no matter who they are." We can put ourselves in jeopardy if we insulate our lives from correction. Our use of the gifts of the Spirit does not mature without loving correction and outside input. The same applies to our teaching if we insulate ourselves from correction and constructive input; if we do, we will lose our ability to hear the voice of God because our ears have become plugged with the effects of pride. God opposes proud attitudes.

If you are married, your primary source for this

insight will be your spouse. They know you better than anyone on earth. If your marriage is healthy, you will allow for this kind of free and open communication. Friends who know God's heart and are allowed to speak into your life will also be able to help you see the larger picture. And then there are the people who approach you, like the woman who left our church or any little old lady who knows her Bible; even though these people bring correction outside of a trusted relationship, it can carry the heart of God. Don't dismiss these people, because the word they bring may be a pivotal point in your training.

No matter how mature you become in the gift of prophecy, you never want to set yourself above receiving corrective insight. You need some of these corrections to insure your ability to continue speaking for God over the long run. A teachable spirit is one of the most powerful manifestations of Holy Spirit's work in your life.

PROPHETIC PRINCIPLE
CHALLENGING TERRITORY

All kingdoms are defined by territory. This territory can be defined by the borders of an individual life, a segment of a community, or an entire culture. Kingdoms wield authority by what they are able to possess, control, and influence. The primary territory any ruler seeks to govern is the will of the people who live within the boundaries of his realm. The submitted will of the populace gives the ruler authority to release his will on the population. In God's Kingdom we call this Lordship. In hell's kingdom we call it control and bondage.

Once the will of an individual yields to the authority of the kingdom of darkness, what follows will be the submission of families, political systems, and nations to a dark agenda. A prophetic word will breach the border of these dark domains and challenge their authority and right to exist. When this happens there will be a reaction.

The Book of Acts describes several of these kingdom conflicts. For example, Paul was arrested in Philippi for casting a demon out of a young woman who was bringing great wealth to her handlers through her demonic practice of fortune telling. Her deliverance shook the financial stability of a city. The reaction was swift and violent. Paul and Silas were arrested, beaten, and thrown into prison. God used that entire event to set the demon-possessed girl free, save the household of the jailer, and build the faith of a praying church. God wastes none of our negative experiences.

When you speak a prophetic word into a place of bondage, you will threaten the territorial right of hell to possess a life or a cultural institution. In these moments of revelation, a prophetic word becomes a spiritual pry bar to help release the grip of deception holding people captive.

This process of deliverance makes the kingdom of darkness nervous. Hell will use any and all means to silence your voice, including threats, accusation or dismissal: these are the desperate tactics of a kingdom in jeopardy.

CHAPTER 11
THE POWER OF A SINGLE WORD

When Jan and I lived in Europe, part of our assignment was to travel throughout the countries and discover what God was doing in various nations by meeting with pastors and leaders and establishing relationships with them. We also traveled to visit, strengthen, and encourage our existing family of churches.

A group of churches we worked with held an annual gathering funded by their mother church in the United States. One year, that conference was suspended. Jan asked me if some of the conference funds could be used to create a retreat with the primary leaders from each nation. This would give us all some quality time together.

I got permission to use some of the funds to take the primary leadership couple from each nation on a three-day retreat. We could leave behind the demands of everyday life and simply be refreshed and restored as we listened to the Lord. It wasn't a time of fasting or being monastic. It was to be a time of feasting and laughter. Many of these leaders had no way to fund such a break from their own resources, so this plan turned out to be something special.

The Lord gave us distinct instructions to have no

agenda—no plan for our time away. This was a time of rest with a heavenly purpose. We asked the Lord for one word or one sentence that would steer each leader's heart and their nation. Without exception, the Lord spoke to each leader either a word of affirmation, encouragement, or direction.

Some of these conversations dealt with a fear that limited a leader's scope of influence. One leader confessed a sin he kept hidden in fear of losing his ministry. Others were encouraged by a simple sentence of hope dropped into our conversation during a shared meal.

One couple had limited their vision to just the region of the country where they grew up, even though they were national leaders. They were faithful and fruitful in that place of familiarity. The church they pastored was impacting their immediate region, but it had little effect in the cities beyond—especially in the nation's capital. While in conversation during a meal, the wife commented that they could never reach the nation's capitol. It was too far away. They had no one to send. They did not have the funds.

I simply said, "With God all things are possible. We will pray and dream with you and see what God will do." There was no discernible change in the attitude of this couple, but the Spirit made a deposit of truth that confronted an embedded lie. Under the control of Communism, people had not been allowed to travel freely. The ability to dream beyond one's immediate region had been shut down.

A year later, after we had returned to the United States, we heard that this couple was sending someone to their nation's capital to plant a church. When I heard this news, I remembered what the Lord had spoken during our retreat. I believe that word was part of a process that set such a church plant in motion. One word given by the Spirit had the ability to redirect the destiny of a church movement toward greater Kingdom expansion.

The power and authority of God are not attached to the length of a word or its style of delivery, but to the content of His heart revealed in the word. Each word will sound different but will share a single commonality: each prophetic word is an expression of God's love. Some of the most profound words I have ever received were no more than a single paragraph in length, but each one was infused with God's love.

During those years in Europe, we received far more than we could give out. We experienced a cultural and language barrier in each country we visited. We learned experientially what we knew in our intellect: that we could not rely on our own understanding. Every step had to be Spirit-led. We had no choice but to follow the simple impressions of the Spirit. As a result, we received fresh revelation. The leaders we served were not the only ones encouraged to step beyond the predictable and comfortable patterns of life into something new. God used that time to reform our lives and thinking, too. We left Europe and returned to the United States changed forever.

PROPHETIC PRINCIPLE
DELAYED TESTIMONIES

Recently, I had a few hours of spare time. Just before the lunch hour, I got into my pickup truck and went for a drive to visit some local stores. All morning I had the desire to have a burger and fries. This is not the healthiest of lunch choices, but every once in a while it's OK. I was trying to save gas and started looking for a place to eat near where my errands were taking place. The more I looked, the more a little burger stand about ten miles away kept coming to mind. I realized I needed to follow my instincts and make the drive.

When I arrived at the stand, I noticed a woman sitting at one of the outdoor picnic tables eating her burger and talking with the owner. As I stood waiting for my order, the owner and the woman drew me into their conversation about parenting. After I made a few comments, the woman asked, "Are you a teacher?" I responded with, "Yes, in some ways I am." The conversation moved on. When my order came, I sat at the opposite end of the outdoor table and began to eat my lunch.

After a few minutes, the woman said, "You look familiar. What do you do?" I told her I was the pastor of

Living Waters Church in Medford, Oregon. With that she said, "I knew it. I visited your church years ago with some friends. You gave me a prophetic word, and I never forgot it." She repeated in detail the word I had given her and how much God had used that word to bring order to her life. After my lunch was finished, I drove the ten miles back home feeling that my desire for a burger had involved more than just satisfying my natural hunger pangs.

I share this story to encourage you. Each time you release a prophetic word, you release life. Some of the words you release may not seem to bear visible and immediate fruit. Some of those words are carried back and lived out in a distant time and place. You may not always see the results of what you prophesy, but God will occasionally provide a status report for a word you delivered in the past.

I know I enjoyed hearing that report at the hamburger stand. I also enjoyed the humor: God showed me He can speak to me even through my hunger for lunch.

After all, we carry the very presence of God. Because of that reality, what appears to be a lunch craving might carry the potential of something greater.

CHAPTER 12
YOUR PROPHETIC HISTORY

If you have had prophetic words spoken over you, those words contain elements of your destiny that will be fulfilled somewhere in your future.

I remember the words spoken to me throughout my own life history. Today, Jan and I are living out the elements of those words. Over the years, Jan has faithfully documented the words we've received, and we review them from time to time to build our faith or check to see if we are on track—especially if we are waiting to discover direction for a new season.

We can see the power of prophetic history throughout Scripture. God told Abram to begin moving toward a land he could not see. God spoke to Moses from a burning bush of what was to come. Joshua led the people of God into a land of promise, prophesied in centuries past. Ananias prophesied to Paul his life mission. These people moved forward on a word of promise.

My mother once told me a story I had never heard. When I was a little boy, my grandmother said, "He will be a preacher." Immediately, my mother thought she was referring to my brother, Dwain. My brother is a wonderful man, husband, father, and grandfather. He would make a great pastor, but God took him in another direction. My grandmother corrected my mother by saying, "No, I meant Garris." If you looked at the early trajectory of my life you would probably have come to the same conclusion as my mother. The word my grandmother spoke remained unfulfilled for years before it became my reality.

God will often release an assignment before a person is ready to partner with His plan. Later in life, once the connection is made, the word becomes a confirmation. My mother shared this story with me when I had been pastoring for several years. She forgot about it and remembered it in a season when I needed encouragement and confirmation that God had called me to shepherd His people.

God deposits prophetic treasures into our historical timeline that we will discover, incrementally, throughout our lifetime. That word from my grandmother was prophesied forward into my future while I was still a child. Later, it became a powerful affirmation in a challenging season of my life.

Collect your prophetic history. Revisit these words from time to time to see if the life you are living is aligned with the promises of God spoken over you somewhere in your past. These words can become a course correction or the reengagement of promise you had previously abandoned. Understanding your prophetic history will help you fulfill your destiny and calling.

PROPHETIC PRINCIPLE
BRINGING A WORD OF CORRECTION

One of the most challenging things we can do is to bring a word of correction. Hopefully, these corrective words are birthed only by a merciful work of the Spirit and not by our own impatience or frustration.

Perpetually, angry prophets who are upset with broken people and a broken culture are often dealing with unresolved personal issues that fuel the angry words they speak. These angry attitudes and harsh methods of delivery can sound spiritual to those who share a similar anger, but they do not reflect the heart of God.

There is a safeguard that will keep you from joining with an angry chorus. When you find you are being asked to bring a word of correction, allow that word to first pass through your own life. Discover where it might apply to you. This process of self-examination will surround the corrective word with a merciful attitude, content, and method of delivery. When you recognize your own need for God's mercy, you will be careful how you represent Him to others.

Chapter 13
BREAD FROM HEAVEN

When I pastored a local church, I received a report from our bookkeeper each week letting me know the amount of our Sunday offerings. Part of the reality of leadership in a church is having ministries to fund and bills to pay. One week when I read the report, I was humbled at the level of giving from our church, considering the condition of the world economy at the time. I went back into my office, got down on my knees, and thanked God for His goodness. I thanked Him for the people in our church who were learning how to walk in new levels of faithfulness and generosity.

I got up and crafted an email to our financial council to share with them the wonderful thing God was doing in our finances. We were seeing financial provision that was exceeding the projections of our monthly budget. We couldn't figure out why this was taking place. It was simply God doing something the world's economy said should not be happening.

As I sat at my desk typing the email, I heard a loud thud against my office door—like someone had thrown something against it. My office faced a busy street and is on one of the main roads leading to a large high school adjacent to our church property. I thought the thud against the door was some act of youthful exuberance or a prank.

I got up and opened my office door to look for the prankster. No one was there. Then I looked down. There on my doorstep was a pizza crust: a big one. It wasn't there when I arrived at the office a few minutes earlier.

Immediately, I looked up in time to see a large crow flying away. I am guessing the crow had carried the pizza crust through the air and dropped it, striking my office door. The crow was a really good bomber because he would have had to release a perfectly timed shot to make it over the bushes and under the roofline of the overhanging porch. The pizza crust fell through the only slot of open airspace to make its delivery. If fact, dropping the pizza crust and having it hit my door resembled the accuracy of a laser-guided bomb.

All of this—the door opening, my looking down and seeing the pizza crust and the crow flying off—took place in just a few seconds. As I collected my thoughts, the Lord reminded me of Elijah who was told by God to go to the Kerith Ravine and wait. Elijah was told he would supernaturally be provided for.

In 1 Kings 17:3-5 the text says:

"Go to the east and hide by Kerith Brook, near where it enters the Jordan River. Drink from the brook and eat what the ravens bring you, for I have commanded them to bring you food." So Elijah did as the LORD told him and camped beside Kerith Brook, east of the Jordan.

A few months prior, the Lord spoke to me about a supernatural provision He was bringing to our church—a provision that could not be understood or explained with the natural mind. The event with the crow and its incredible accuracy in dropping the pizza crust at my office door was beginning to make sense.

God can use something natural to confirm a spiritual truth. The crow dropping the pizza crust against my office door got my attention. What God used to get my attention was not the word itself. It simply caused me to focus on Him to hear what He wanted to say.

Within every circumstance God uses to get our attention is a message. Not all of these are words to share with other people. Many of them are simply words of comfort to remind us that God is at work. These events also teach us that God can use anything in His creation to grab our attention, even a crow with a well-timed release of a pizza crust.

Prophetic Principle
YOU NEVER PROPHESY COMPLETE REVELATION

Now our knowledge is partial and incomplete, and even the gift of prophecy reveals only part of the whole picture.—I Corinthians 13:9

When Paul penned these words, he was sharing a principle for prophetic ministry. He was also sharing a principle for life. Nothing we do or say is ever the complete or final word on any subject. Whenever you bring a prophetic word, it only reveals part of a much larger picture. To think we bring complete revelation is both naïve and arrogant. Such assumptions also reveal a lack of understanding about how the gift of prophecy actually functions.

Most people who hear a prophetic word will respond graciously with a welcoming heart. A small percentage may get upset or anxious because what you spoke did not bring complete understanding or filter easily through their theological grid. Prophetic ministry is full of these varied reactions.

When someone confronts you and challenges the

content of your message, they may simply need a gentle and private response from you. A gracious interaction with them has the potential to ease their displeasure and provide them an opportunity to consider a more compassionate and measured response in the future. For those who continue in their angry correction, bless them and move on. Your response, no matter how gracious, will actually fuel their negative attitude, giving them a wider audience where they can vent their anger.

Whenever you open your mouth and speak in God's name, you will always run the risk of experiencing someone's displeasure. Don't give up or get defensive. Use that experience to develop the depth of your character and the maturity of your gifting.

CHAPTER 14
CHANGING NAMES

After four years in Europe, Jan and moved back to Oregon to pastor a local church. When we stepped off the plane, we carried almost everything we owned in our luggage. Our return meant we were literally starting over.

One of the first things we needed was a vehicle. We found a nice Chevy Blazer on a used car lot in Portland and drove it south to our new home in Medford.

Our assignment was to pastor a church called Faith Bible Center. When I first heard the name of the church, it didn't impress me one way or another. That was the church God asked us to lead, and that was the name.

Shortly after our arrival, a man in the church handed me a cassette tape he wanted me to hear (yes, it was that long ago!). The tape's subject did not interest me at the time, so I put it in the Blazer's glove box and forgot about it.

We were invited to meet the leadership team of our high school youth group. They were staying in a private cabin for a retreat on the shores of Lake of the Woods. This lake is stunning. It is like a jewel placed in the setting of the Cascade Mountains with the sentinel of Mount

McLoughlin reflecting its snow-capped summit across the surface of the water.

Meeting new friends was lots of fun. We spent the afternoon listening to their hearts and the vision God had given them for the youth of our valley. When our meeting was finished, we drove back to Medford.

On our drive home, we decided to take the long way back down the Green Springs Highway to enjoy the beautiful mountain scenery. It seemed like a good time to listen to the tape, so I pulled it out of the glove box, slipped it into the cassette player, and we listened to it as we drove down the mountain.

When the message was finished, the voice of a professional announcer came on to offer products for sale similar to the subject addressed by the speaker. At the very end of the announcement the man said, "As you listen to this tape, a river of living waters will begin to flow out of you." At that moment the Lord said to me, "That is the new name of Faith Bible Center. You are to change the name to Living Waters."

When I heard what the Lord had asked me to do, I turned to share it with Jan. Before I could open my mouth she said, "I heard it too—it is Living Waters!" We drove on for the next few moments in silence as we pondered the profound clarity with which the Lord had just spoken. We knew we were experiencing a divine moment.

We had not been in Medford for more than a month, and now the Lord was asking us to do something that could have significant repercussions if not handled well. Not only that, we always had clear instruction from the Lord to enter a new place of ministry as "historians and lovers." We were not there to push our own agenda. Our goal was to learn the history of this church and love the people well before making any major decisions. This decision would effect generations to come. We wanted to walk with wisdom.

For some people, asking to change the name of their church is like asking permission to change the name of their firstborn child. Having coached pastors and churches in the past, I always advised that these kinds of major changes be made only after years of building up a great deal of relational trust equity. Yet here we were, the brand new pastors, getting ready to obey an instruction from the Lord that could really shake things up.

We began to process how to proceed. I knew the actual change would take several months to accomplish. Over time, I went to every past leader, every current leader, and any one who had leadership potential, and shared the story surrounding the proposed name change. In the following weeks, I would talk with no less than thirty people and—to a person—each one said, in essence, "This is God. Do it!"

The last person I had planned to talk with was a dear woman considered by many to be the spiritual mother of the church. Her presence and opinion carried significant authority in the lives of many people. If the name change were to be opposed by this spiritual mother, it would present a challenge. Jan and I had an appointment to meet with her and her husband in their home to offer our comfort, prayer, and encouragement because her husband was very ill.

At the end of our visit, I shared the story about the proposed name change. Tears began to well up in the woman's eyes. At first, I thought her tears were tears of sorrow at the prospect of changing the name of her beloved church. I asked her to tell me what she was feeling.

She began to smile as the tears tracked down her face. She said, "Garris, two weeks ago during worship, I looked out over the congregation. As I watched, the people became jars. Some were partially full and others were empty. I saw the Lord enter the sanctuary with a large container of water on His shoulder. He began to pour the water into each vessel. Then He said, 'I am going to make this a place of living waters.'" When I heard that prophetic image, I knew the name change was a done deal. God was prophetically confirming the change beyond the initial instructions He had revealed to us on our drive home from Lake of the Woods.

We began talking with our leadership team about when to announce the proposed name change and take the vote that would approve the change. Our particular family of churches requires a vote for the name change of a church. That vote would then be given to the governing board of our movement for their final approval. In the intervening weeks, the church had begun to grow, requiring us to add a second service. We set a date for a Sunday in early December to bring the proposed name change before the church for a vote.

That Sunday morning, something wonderful and affirming took place. After asking for a show of hands from the people to approve the name change, we did not have one vote to the negative. We had 100% affirmation. We entered the New Year under a new name with a new and hope-filled future.

If you are going to see significant change in your life or the lives of other people, don't begin the journey until you have a word from the Lord. Inquire of the Lord about everything. Bringing change without a word from the Lord will have you creating change out of human logic and wisdom. Neither carries the power of a word spoken from God.

God knows how challenging change can be for all of us. He gives us prophetic words to encourage us to take the first step forward. With each step, He will encourage other people to join us in the journey because they know God has spoken.

PROPHETIC PRINCIPLE
SPEAK WORDS SEASONED WITH MERCY

One of God's most profound character traits is His mercy. For God to step through the curtain of time and interact with frail and broken humanity required mercy. Mercy meets people at the place of their greatest need and embraces them with words of hope.

To be effective in God's Kingdom requires a heart of mercy. This heart is developed in people who have not forgotten the original mercy God extended to them. Whenever our words become distanced from this recollection, it is too easy to speak in flippant and unloving ways. Our words can become verbal hammers, wounding and bruising people.

In order to defend against this potential abuse, it is important to create a definition of mercy written from within the memory of your greatest failure and eventual restoration. Remembering this experience will keep you honest and real when relating to other broken people. Paul never forgot where he came from. The Road to Damascus was not just a road linking cities—it was a place where a self-righteous and unmerciful Saul was introduced to the holy and merciful God of Heaven.

Throughout all his life, Paul never forgot the mercy God had extended to him. On several occasions he reminded his readers of that mercy. He told his young disciple Timothy, *But God had mercy on me so that Christ Jesus could use me as a prime example of his great patience with even the worst sinners* (I Timothy 1:16).

Before we speak for God, we need to remember what it was like to feel abandoned and then redeemed. We need to recall what it was like to live trapped in sin and what it felt like to finally be set free. A prophetic voice that forgets these realities can turn to judgment. Unmerciful words spoken in the name of God will create confusion in the hearers and grief in the heart of God. Words of mercy will always triumph over words of judgment.

CHAPTER 15
PROPHESYING TO YOURSELF

On a cold and snowy December night, I had to walk down our street to a neighbor's house to retrieve a laptop computer. The surface of the street was a combination of bare pavement and ice. On my return trip home, my right foot slipped on a patch of ice and then suddenly caught on a section of dry pavement. All of my weight came down on my right leg and put so much pressure on my quadriceps tendon that it snapped, dropping me down to the street like someone had hit my leg with a sledgehammer. The pain was excruciating.

It was late in the day, and the sun was setting. The section of roadway where I had fallen is a small connector street without any houses. I needed help, but I was alone. I remembered I had picked up my cell phone prior to leaving the house. I called Jan and uttered a prayer, "Lord, please let Jan hear this call." After a few rings, she picked up the phone. She could tell by my voice I was in trouble. She immediately grabbed her car keys and set out to find me.

As I lay there, a car drove by at the far end of the street about 200 feet away. I saw the car stop, back up, and then turn down the street and head toward me. To this day, I don't know how the driver saw me in the limited light of dusk. He and Jan arrived at the same time. The man helped Jan load me into our car. If Jan had been alone, it would have been very difficult to move me. I still wonder if the man was really an angel sent to help.

Jan drove me to the hospital where a doctor confirmed the nature of my injury. I was fitted with a temporary brace and sent home. Three days later, I was back in the hospital for surgery to reattach my torn tendon.

After surgery and for the next several weeks, I was on strong medication to ease the pain. I was so uncomfortable and restless from the pain and medication that I could not sleep in our bed without waking Jan, so I spent those first few weeks in our living room sleeping on the couch. Jan was such a wonderful nurse to me; I owed her a good night's sleep.

About three weeks after the surgery, the recovery process and powerful medications were beginning to take a toll on me. In the middle of the night, I got up to hobble into our guest bathroom. I was washing my hands and looked up into the mirror. My face looked drawn and pale. I felt weak. I was tired of the recovery process. The thought of having to endure months of rehabilitation was depressing. I wanted my normal life back.

I looked at my miserable image reflecting back at me from the mirror, and something happened that I had never before experienced: I felt despair—overwhelming despair. Immediately, the mirror turned into a movie screen. I saw my life floating down a powerful river toward a huge waterfall. I knew I would soon go over the falls and descend into its depths. I have known people who went over these falls of despair, and some of them never returned. With the despair came a feeling of complete hopelessness.

This oppressive vision continued to unfold, floating

me closer to the edge of the falls. Realizing how spiritually dangerous this situation was, I shouted into the mirror, "I don't have despair! I have God!" Immediately, the image disappeared. My heart began to respond to the words of hope, and the feeling of despair vanished. I began to weep.

When I got back to the couch, the Lord spoke to me and said, "I am leading you to a good place." Those words flooded me with peace. I could leave the outcome of events—and all I had suffered—in the hands of a good God who would lead me to the goodness He had planned for the remainder of my life. This current suffering was not my final destination.

In my time of isolation and recovery, the Lord gave me an assignment. I had planned to write a book about the transitions of life—but not for couple of years. God's timing was more accelerated.

In the weeks ahead, I began writing a book titled, *A Good Place*, birthed out of the revelation of God's goodness. The image of freedom God revealed to me in front of the mirror was the seedbed for the book. That emptiness had been filled with a new revelation of God's heart that has become a valuable word for people who are navigating personal times of transition. God never wastes our sorrows if we will entrust ourselves to Him.

No matter how deep the despair and hopelessness you experience, God will always provide a word of hope to reset the direction of your life. He brings these words and images to us when we need them most. Out of our painful experiences come some of the most profound words God will ever speak to us.

In that dark night in front of the bathroom mirror, when I prophesied the word of hope God had downloaded to me, I was prophesying to myself. There are times when the most powerful prophetic word you will declare is not for someone else, but for yourself.

PROPHETIC PRINCIPLE
AVOID THE INVITATION TO JOIN THE FIGHT

The intensity of certain social issues or the condition of culture can create unrestrained and unwise responses from people—even from those of us who desire to speak for God. In these intense social climates, people want and need answers. When you find yourself in one of these moments, be careful with your words.

Human brokenness and cultural decay do not make Heaven nervous. These have been the human conditions since sin first entered humanity in the Garden. In challenging times, a true prophetic voice will wait for the Lord to provide a message instead of jumping on the latest emotional bandwagon and speaking words designed to tickle impatient ears.

Your voice is not yours alone: it belongs to God. Do not let what you speak be taken hostage by the agenda of others. Avoid the invitation to join a chorus not orchestrated by God. If you are wise enough to do so, then when the current flap and fervor is over and the masses have moved on to the next cultural battle, you will still have your credibility intact.

CHAPTER 16
DEFINING MOMENTS

There may come an experience so painful that it will indelibly mark your life. These events become the before and after point for everything else that follows. Such a marker event can be a divorce, a death of a loved one, or an illness. These painful experiences are not supposed to ultimately define your life. The true definition of your life comes from God and what you allow Him to do in your heart when all hell is breaking loose.

I saw this played out in vivid detail when a friend's wife had an emotional breakdown while he was hundreds of miles away in another state. On the long drive back to his home, hell began painting horrible images of his future and the future of his marriage. He was taken to places in his mind where only dark resolutions lurked. Finally, he had enough and spoke out loud to these deceptive spirits and told them to be silent. He began declaring the words of hope God had previously spoken over his life, his marriage, and his future. When he spoke, the atmosphere in his car was vacuumed of the lies illegally hitching a ride with him back to his home.

My friend tenderly and compassionately met his wife

in her time of need and rallied support and help. In the days following, life began to stabilize, but the lies that initiated the breakdown were still speaking death and despair to his wife. After three weeks, he realized he needed to address the lies still present in his home. He repeated the same rebuke he had spoken to the darkness that filled his car. Those words of hope and promise broke the power of a lie that wanted to take up residence and fill his home with its deceptive presence.

It was as if a light flipped on in his home and in the mind of his wife. Over the ensuing months, friends and professional counselors helped her learn how to reorder her life and continue living in freedom.

It is far too easy to allow painful events to become a destination of despair and hopelessness. If we are not on guard, we can become so overwhelmed that we exchange our true identity and heritage for a lie. Words of hope from God confront these lies and displace their negative presence.

No matter where you are in your journey as a believer, you are always defined by resurrection. If resurrection is not present in your current situation you do not yet have a full understanding of what is true. Your life is always defined as a rising, never a descent. When you face moments of personal tragedy, your part in the recovery process will be to declare light into dark places and speak life to what seems dead. Resurrection is your ultimate destination no matter where the events of your life seem to be leading.

This is the nature of prophecy. A word of the Lord calls people to life and hope. Even a corrective word brings life. Your words of truth and love contain the power of God to set the captive free from pits of darkness and from the convincing lies of deceiving spirits.

The way of the righteous is like the first gleam of

dawn, which shines ever brighter until the full light of day (Proverbs 4:18).

PROPHETIC PRINCIPLE
KEEP IT SIMPLE

A prophetic word from God sets in motion the potential of breakthrough in a person's life. These words do not always carry with them the detailed instructions needed to walk out each step of the journey. Remember to resist the urge to speak beyond the initial scope of the word you were given; don't fill in the blanks.

The word you deliver is not a complete picture. The person receiving a prophetic word will need to exercise belief in order to activate the word's potential. At the point of belief, they enter into a partnership and agreement with God to bring about the word's fulfillment. The blanks in a prophetic word are where the recipient will be asked to trust God to make known what still remains a mystery. You need to be sensitive to the Spirit in these times and know when to step back. God is the one who promises to fulfill what He has spoken, not those who bring a prophetic word.

If someone struggles with the implications of what was spoken or they need wisdom on how to respond, these are moments when they begin to learn what it means to struggle well. This is a struggle that moves them deeper into a place of trust with God.

The Spirit will be faithful to bring understanding once a word has been activated by faith. We must choose to believe and obey even though we don't have all the facts or a known destination in sight.

Chapter 17
RIGHT DIRECTION, WRONG ALTITUDE

Early one morning, an experienced pilot and two of his friends took off from a small Montana airport to fly across the Rocky Mountains. This ill-fated flight disappeared from the radar screen within minutes of departure. Something went terribly wrong, and the airplane crashed. Later in the day, a search helicopter discovered the aircraft wreckage embedded at the top of a mountain ridge. All aboard had perished.

I was familiar with this particular airport and the flight path of this fatal crash because, as a young pastor, I augmented our family income as a flight instructor and charter pilot. I had flown in and out of this particular airport many times.

The flight would have been routine for that experienced pilot. But the morning of the trip, the entire valley and the tops of the surrounding mountains were covered in clouds. In order to safely depart, a pilot would need to file an instrument flight plan, enabling him to fly up and through the cloud cover to get on top.

Each aircraft has an instrument that tells a pilot how

high he is flying. This instrument, called an altimeter, is pressure sensitive and reads altitude based on barometric pressure. An altimeter needs to be adjusted to the current pressure readings for each flight segment to make sure you are flying at a precise altitude. If you miss this one item on your checklist and fail to make the proper adjustments, you could actually be flying lower than your instruments are telling you. This kind of mistake can get you killed if mountains are hidden in the clouds.

Somewhere in the process of a hurried departure, this experienced pilot missed one thing on his checklist. He failed to adjust his altimeter. Crash investigators discovered this when they examined wreckage from the crash site.

A few years after that incident, I was hiking near the top of the Rocky Mountains that overlook the Flathead Valley in Northwest Montana. These mountains are like a beautiful necklace surrounding the valley.

I was hiking along at the timberline in an alpine zone where vegetation and trees thin out, and the ridgeline is mostly rock and gravel. Ahead of me, I saw a dark stain in the soil measuring about six feet across. In and around the stain were bits of shattered aluminum and small shards of twisted aircraft wreckage. I realized I had come upon a crash site. From my vantage point, I could mentally calculate the route of an instrument flight departure from the airport in the valley below, and I knew this was the crash site of the three men who had perished a few years before.

I walked over to the oil stain and paused. This was a place where three men had been talking and laughing one moment, and in the next moment they entered eternity unexpectedly. I was standing on sacred ground.

After a few moments of reflection, I started to investigate the crash site. I began digging through the oil stain left behind from the fragmented aircraft engine. As I dug deeper into the oily soil, I discovered parts of the aircraft's instruments—the very ones the pilot had relied on to direct his flight path.

I stood looking up to the top of the ridgeline. The impact point of the crash was only six feet below the top of the mountain. The difference between life and death was only six feet. Failing to adjust the altimeter to the local barometric pressure had been a fatal error. This crash site had much to say about how we are to live our lives and how we are to use the gifts God has given us.

When you prophesy, every word you offer will have an atmosphere in which it will be delivered. Like a pilot who needs to constantly reset his altimeter to the changing levels of barometric pressure, you are wise to intentionally get reset by the Spirit before you speak.

There will be times when you are speaking into situations where you are surrounded by the clouds of a circumstance so thick you cannot see where your word is going. Let God, not the circumstance, determine what you do and how you speak. Even a slight, Spirit-inspired adjustment in your attitude or your method of delivery can make the difference between rising to the level of the word's intended purpose or crashing into the unseen obstacles God intended you to clear.

Prophetic Principle
Seeing Through Prophetic Prisms

When Jan and I got engaged, we went to a jewelry store in a local mall to purchase our rings. We selected wedding bands for both of us and an engagement ring for Jan. We were not well off financially, so the diamond set in Jan's ring was small, but it was special for us.

After forty-two years, we wear those same rings on our fingers—minus Jan's diamond. Years ago, the diamond loosened from its setting and was lost. Jan now wears her mother's ring with its diamond held securely in place. Our wedding bands used to have a design imprinted on their surface, but after all the years of daily wear, those designs have worn away.

A diamond is different. Diamonds are like prophetic words. They resist the wear of time, and—even after many years—they look as beautiful as the day they were first placed on your finger.

A cut diamond is unique. When light passes through its different angles, the prism of the stone provides a singular perspective on the diamond's beauty. To more fully appreciate a diamond, we turn the stone around in our hand to catch these different angles of light. Each new angle provides a new perspective.

When you speak prophetically, you are speaking from a place of perspective. Your perspective is never a comprehensive view. You will only see a partial reflection of something much larger. With this in mind, don't assume that everyone will fully appreciate what you share from your place of limited perspective. Deliver the word God gives you, and allow people to view it in their own way, from their unique place of perspective. They will see something different from what you see. Their view will put a new light on the revelation God has given. The gift of prophecy is like a multifaceted gem waiting to reflect the beauty of God.

Chapter 18
WHEN GOD GETS OUR ATTENTION

I was in my office at church when a dove landed on the sidewalk just outside my window. I like doves, so I got up from my desk, went to the window, and spent some time watching the bird.

The next day, the dove showed up again. This went on for the better part of a week, every day. Toward the end of the week, I finally asked the Lord, "Is there something here you are trying to say to me?" In an instant, I heard the Lord speak to my heart, "Invite my peace into the church." This invitation seemed like an unusual request since there were no major issues taking place in the church at the time. In fact, it was a great season of God's manifest presence in our church. However, in simple obedience I said, "Lord, I invite your peace into this church." I felt that my simple prayer was a deposit for our future.

The next Saturday morning, I was driving to the church like I did each week. The Lord asked me to arrive early every Saturday to be alone with Him in preparation for our Sunday morning services. The other pastors honored this time for me to be alone with God, so I had the sanctuary and the facility all to myself. I could walk around and pray loudly, or I could lay in silence before the Lord, uninterrupted. I treasured this time.

I usually arrived at the church by 4:30 a.m. There was never a need to set an alarm for this day of the week because the Lord would always wake me. I think He loved this time with me so much that He nudged awake just to be with Him.

The sunrise was still an hour away when I arrived at the church. My headlights illuminated a lone dove nesting in the middle of the parking lot. I stopped my car and looked at the dove. Instead of standing, the dove had nestled down and made itself comfortable. This is unusual for any bird because they are vulnerable to predators on the ground.

The dove and I sat and stared at each other. The Lord spoke again, "I am bringing my peace into the dark and fearful places in people's lives." As soon as I heard those words, the dove rose to its legs, flapped its wings, and flew off into the dark. This got my attention because I was coming to the office that morning to finalize a message on finding the peace of God in the dark places of life.

A few days after the dove incident in the parking lot, I arrived at the church on a regular workday. The sun was already bright in the eastern sky. Our pastors were meeting that morning to pray before the office opened. I had begun to turn into the church parking lot when I stopped in surprise. Just above the driveway entrance to our parking lot were ten doves, all bunched together on a telephone wire immediately above me. I counted them: ten—all pressed together, side by side.

After I parked the car and got out to look again, the ten doves had flown away. I couldn't get this last group of doves out of my mind. In my office, I pulled out a reference book and checked into what the number ten might mean and to refresh my understanding on the symbol of a dove. I knew a dove was a symbol of peace and life, but I sensed there was more to this incident.

One of the meanings for the number ten is "testimony." The Lord spoke and said, "I am going to give you something to testify about!" A new level of expectation rose up in me that God was bringing to our church and community something to testify about.

I began to have more clarity on a couple of things. I was in a season where I was more sensitive to God than normal. I was more open to Him speaking to me through the natural and everyday events of life. As a result, I didn't dismiss things like the doves appearing. After all, God created these animals, and He could use them to get my attention.

The doves were not the message. The word of the Lord that followed the dove's appearance was the message God wanted me to hear. As beautiful as the doves were, the word of the Lord is far more magnificent. His word, not what He uses to get our attention, is the message.

We never want to get so busy that we become numb to the voice of God trying to speak to us through the happenings of daily life. If you are going to be used by God to transmit His truth, you need to remain sensitive to the world around you. God can speak through any aspect of His creation.

A funny side note: just a week after all the dove appearances, I was driving to an appointment. All of a sudden, a dove appeared and began to fly right next to my driver's side window. I must have been doing 30 miles per hour. The dove paced himself with my car for a moment— a moment long enough for me to be reminded that God had spoken those previous words to me about peace. Once I remembered, the dove flew away. God didn't want me to forget what He said.

Take a moment, look around, and view your surroundings. God may be trying to get your attention through the unfolding circumstances of your life in this very moment. Living in anticipation that God is always communicating with you in some form or fashion will change how you see and interpret everyday events.

Prophetic Principle
HIJACKED MEANING

I have had people attempt to hijack what I've said by taking the content of my words and reinterpreting my intent to reflect their opinion. In a world where immediate social media interaction is always available, this can happen with ease and speed.

It is dangerous to try and correct each and every one of these misinterpretations. If you are not careful, you can be drawn into heated and overly corrective public conversations. You want God's original intent—not a divisive interaction with those who challenge your words.

Paul addressed this when he wrote to Timothy:

> *Again I say, don't get involved in foolish, ignorant arguments that only start fights. A servant of the Lord must not quarrel but must be kind to everyone, be able to teach, and be patient with difficult people* (2 Timothy 2:23-24).

At first, it will be hard to walk away and leave these arguments alone. You will want to defend yourself. Learn the wisdom of silence.

CHAPTER 19
CHANGING YOUR CONTEXT

I was in the middle of a writing project when I experienced something I call "revelation block." I'm not talking about writer's block, when you can't write. Revelation block is when you need to hear something from the Lord before you attempt to write another word. I never wanted to write just to produce more articles and books. I have always wanted to write from a place of revelation. So when I have a block, I need to deal with it.

I got up from my computer, put on my hiking shoes, and walked into the hills that surround our home. The trails that lace these hills have always been my place of refuge, retreat, and revelation. While walking these trails, I have no agenda apart from being present with the Lord. My only assignment is to listen.

About an hour into this change of environment, the words that eluded me finally came with clarity and simplicity. I stopped and recorded what God had shared. I took that revelation back to my computer and picked up my writing project where I had left off.

Environment is important. There are times when we continue to wait in a context where the word we seek is not intended to come. Some of us linger too long thinking that productivity will produce what we desire. This is not always true.

Jesus changed His everyday context from time to time. He went to the garden. He walked in a wilderness. He stood atop the Mount of Transfiguration. Jesus was never enslaved to a single location, and wherever He went, He listened for the Father's voice.

If you are not hearing what you need to hear, you might just need to get up and move. Change your location and your function. You have permission to interrupt the norm. God has things to say to you, and He may want to say them under the trees of a forest or along an unexplored street in your neighborhood. Follow His voice. The revelation you seek is waiting for you.

Prophetic Principle
WHEN A WORD IS NOT RECEIVED

There are reasons why someone may not receive a prophetic word. For example, the content of the word may have been correct, but you simply missed God's timing. Or the hearers of the word may not have the ears to hear what was spoken, and they end up rejecting what they did not understand. But the most challenging reason of all? The word may not be from God.

The last reason is a hard one. This error happens to everyone who is honest enough to admit it. None of us likes to declare, "The Lord says...." and then realize God wasn't saying what we so confidently proclaimed. Some people who do not understand the gift of prophecy in the New Covenant context will call out the Old Covenant stone throwers when they discover your error. They feel it is their assignment to stone to death your mistake. Don't buy into these demands for your premature death.

When a word is not received, give God time to speak to you and reveal the reason why. Mistakes are part of the maturing process we all go through as we learn how to speak with a prophetic voice. God loves people who make mistakes. He loves your risk-taking acts of faith. He is not insecure when you fail.

As you yield to the Spirit, you will experience an increase in your ability to cultivate and hear the distinct difference between your voice and the voice of God— between His timing and yours. With your teachable heart, God will be able to develop your gift into a trustworthy tool for His Kingdom and a weapon to destroy the works of darkness.

Practice the discipline of not taking a negative response personally. Practice becoming someone not easily offended. When a word is not received, don't let your pride get the best of you and keep you from contending for more. Give your defensiveness to God and let Him have His way with your heart and emotions.

Chapter 20
HONORING THE OLD ROADS

There are times when I simply need to "hike it out." A few times each year, I get in one of those mental places where showing up at my office only complicates things. Getting away from everything and everybody and connecting with God in nature helps me clear my mind and hear His voice.

I arrived at the French Gulch Trailhead parking lot at about nine in the morning. After putting on my daypack, I connected with the Payette Trail and began to hike along the south side of Applegate Lake. This lake is located near the California border in Southern Oregon. I wanted to get away from the empty parking lot and civilization as fast as possible. God wanted to talk to me, and I wanted to hear from Him.

I rounded one hillside, and the trail opened up to a panoramic view across the lake. The water lay still in the windless, morning hours. Flocks of waterfowl created small wakes in the distance as they glided across the surface of the water.

Applegate Lake is a manmade reservoir, and the water surface was down by at least a hundred feet. It was the lowest water level in the lake I had ever seen. The descending dirt shoreline resembled little stair steps created as the water receded and etched the shoreline in its descent.

The Applegate Lake wasn't always here. Before the dam, a small town called Copper existed in the bottom of the canyon. Copper had a store and a post office that ran from 1924 to 1932. I can only imagine how nice it was to have the town of Copper way out here in the middle of nowhere, especially when a miner or a homesteading family needed some provisions or wanted to mail a letter. Today, only fish swim along its submerged streets. Boats carrying fishermen buzz along, hundreds of feet above the abandoned town.

As I looked at the water's edge, I noticed an old paved roadway, only visible because of the low water level. Curious, I hiked down the edge of the lake toward the exposed section of roadway.

I began to wonder about the people who had once traveled that road, and the Lord began to have a conversation with me.

He reminded me of an ancient rock pile left at the edge of the Jordan River. That rock pile served as a memorial to future generations of a miraculous river crossing when God took the nation of Israel across the Jordan River and into the Promised Land:

When all the people had crossed the Jordan, the LORD said to Joshua, "Now choose twelve men, one from each tribe. Tell them, 'Take twelve stones from the very place where the priests are standing in the middle of the Jordan. Carry them out and pile them up at the place where you will camp tonight.'" So Joshua called together the twelve men he had chosen — one from each of the tribes of Israel. He told them, "Go into the middle of the Jordan, in front of the Ark of the LORD your God. Each of you must pick up one stone and carry it out on your shoulder—twelve stones in all, one for each of the twelve tribes of Israel. We will use these stones to build a memorial. In the future your children will ask you, 'What do these stones mean?' Then you can tell them, 'They remind us that the Jordan River stopped flowing when the Ark of the LORD's Covenant went across.' These stones will stand as a memorial among the people of Israel forever" (Joshua 4:1-7).

In the years after that crossing, I can imagine Jewish children standing around that pile of rocks and talking about the exploits of Joshua and those who traveled with him into the Promised Land. They would look at these rocks, wondering how in the world an entire nation could cross the watery barrier of the Jordan River on dry ground. They were reminded of the miraculous ways of God.

Underneath the moving waters of the Jordan River was the evidence of a supernatural roadway. This picture is a powerful aspect of prophetic words: they can remind us of the roadways traveled by faith in the past and give us encouragement to believe similar roadways will guide our journey into the future.

Later that morning, I climbed back up the shoreline of the lake and hiked back to my truck, ready to face the present because I had paid a visit to the past.

Prophetic Principle
INCOMPLETE REVELATION

A prophetic word is only a snapshot of a much larger reality. We see in part and we prophesy in part.

You are only an agent of delivery, not the creator of content. Some words will appear to be fragments of something much larger. God has reasons why He does not always give you the full picture. In some cases, He is calling and engaging other people to be part of the process of revelation. They will bring the elements required to create the full picture of what God wants a person to see.

I was spending time with a man I ministered with when suddenly I saw one word appear as though typed on his forehead: *Treachery.* No other description or explanation followed. Until I had further direction, all I could do was intercede. It was not something to discuss with him or anyone except my wife—since we are free to tell each other everything within the scope of honor, and we trust each other implicitly.

I could not act on the word other than to be fully aware and forewarned. There was no visible indication of treachery. Jan and I parked the word because we had no further instructions from the Lord. We took this course because we wanted to view this friend through the lens of mercy. We continued to intercede.

A couple of years later, all the pieces of this painful puzzle came together. The word *treachery* was accurate and heartbreaking. We continued to make the choice to forgive, bless, and release our friend. The Lord eventually brought that experience to a place of restoration.

Resist the urge take a step of premature action or to go beyond the simplicity of a word's original content in an attempt to make it more understandable. This could actually complicate what God wants to do in all involved parties. Hear the word, trust God, and leave it alone until you have further instruction.

Chapter 21

FINDING PURPOSE IN SHAME AND HUMILIATION

I was afraid to start junior high school. My friends and I had heard the horror stories about the "big kids" who didn't like little guys. We heard stories about getting our pants pulled down in front of girls and other tales of juvenile terror. Most of my fears never took place.

The first month of junior high seemed to go by without much of a problem, so I began to think I might have successfully made it through the dreaded initiation.

Each morning all the kids who were bussed to school were required to meet in the cafeteria and wait until class started. I was never really sure why we were not allowed to play on the playground, but I was just a kid. What did I know?

There were rules for all of us held captive in the cafeteria each morning. No talking and no eating were allowed. Our lives were reduced to a very abnormal activity for children our age: motionlessness.

One morning, while riding on the school bus, a kid gave me a stick of gum. I chewed the life out of the gum on the ride to school and forgot it was in my mouth. Upon my arrival in the cafeteria, I was oblivious to the fact that I was breaking one of the cafeteria commandments.

Each morning a teacher would be assigned to monitor our pre-class holding cell in the cafeteria. On this particular morning Mr. Jones (I have changed his name just in case he might still be alive) was the teacher assigned to cafeteria duty. He was a handsome man. All the girls liked him, and they would gather around him. To the guys, it was kind of sickening since we were no competition for Mr. Jones. At this stage in our development we were only skinny/fat/tall/short little nerdy kids who had not fully navigated the confusing season in life called puberty.

About ten minutes into our cafeteria time, I was minding my own business when the really deep and manly voice of Mr. Jones boomed out and echoed off the cement walls and linoleum floors of the cafeteria. Whenever Mr. Jones spoke like this, we knew he was about to emotionally fillet some poor kid. All of us sucked in our collective breath and wondered who would get it this morning.

"You, over there—chewing the gum—look at me!" I was so glad it wasn't me, until I realized I was still chewing the gum given to me on the bus forty-five minutes earlier. He had to be talking about someone else so I didn't look up. Mr. Jones bellowed again, "You, Elkins, look at me!"

At that moment, the thing a junior high kid most dreaded was happening: I was being noticed. A couple of things began to happen. I wanted to go to the bathroom really bad but held it. My bowels were doing those funny things that happen when you are home sick with the flu and need to find a toilet really fast. On the other end of my physiological reaction was the desire to heave up the oatmeal mom made for me earlier that morning, along with the toast, the glass of milk, and the cookie I snuck out of the cookie jar.

As my eyes met the gaze of Mr. Jones, he said, "Yeah, you, Elkins, stand up." As I slowly rose, the entire cafeteria went silent. Junior high kids were about to witness a public execution, so being quiet and obedient was essential for their personal survival.

My life, all twelve years of it, was now flashing before my eyes. Grown-ups said this happens just before a person is about to die, and they were right. Then the snickers started coming from all across the cafeteria. I was being abandoned and left alone in the greatest moment of shame I had ever experienced. It was about to get much worse.

Mr. Jones issued a command, "Elkins, I want you to get down on all fours and crawl over to me like a dog." What? I wanted to protest but only knew I needed to obey the teacher. Slowly I got down on the dirty cafeteria floor and began to crawl on all fours toward Mr. Jones. The kid's snickers had now become outright laughter. Mr. Jones seemed to be feeding off his audience like a comedian working a room. As I crawled toward Mr. Jones, my hands and knees became soiled from the dirt and grease on the floor.

My long and humiliating journey toward Mr. Jones took a couple of minutes to make. It felt like a lifetime. I wanted to hide. I wanted to disappear. I wanted to die.

As I finally came to a stop at the feet of Mr. Jones, he issued another command. "Elkins, crawl over to that garbage can and spit out your gum." In a numbed response of obedience, I crawled over to the garbage can and spit out my gum. At least this torture and humiliation was over, I thought. but Mr. Jones was not done with me.

"Now, get back down on the floor and crawl back to your seat." Again, I crawled in humiliation back across the dirty floor and through the mocking laughter of my classmates. When I reached my seat, I sat down. I was emotionally destroyed. As a kid, I felt my life was over. I had no idea how to get out of the hole Mr. Jones had dug for me. For the rest of the day I existed in an emotional state of numbness. I heard people speaking and felt my feet on the ground, but I was fully disconnected from reality. I was still that way when I got home later that afternoon.

As a family, we always ate dinner together. I was usually the noisy one at the table. On this particular night, I carried my numbness and silence to the dinner table. About half way through our meal, my dad asked me what was wrong. The last thing I wanted to do was recall the events of the day. When I hesitated, dad pressed me to answer because he could see something was terribly wrong.

I spent the next few moments sharing with my family what happened to me. That night I didn't finish my dinner and went off to bed early. The stress of the day had taken a physical toll on my young body, along with the emotional toll on my developing self-image.

Over fifty years have passed since that humiliating incident in the cafeteria. I had parked the pain of that day deep within my heart. Over the years, God had me pray for Mr. Jones. I did not know what to feel about him. As a kid, I was told to respect and trust my elders, yet here was a man who had deeply violated another human being. Today, he would be fired and possibly brought up on charges of child abuse.

As the years went by, I began to add blessings to my prayers for Mr. Jones. I began to prophesy hope and restoration over him.

Somewhere near the forty-year anniversary of that painful event, my wife and I were praying, and this incident came to the surface. I had been traumatized that day, and I needed a spiritual resolution. Jan invited me to pray with her and see what the Lord might say. She prayed "Jesus, come and reveal your truth to Garris."

As I relived my painful crawl across the dirty cafeteria floor, I was shocked to actually see Jesus was with me that day. He was down on all fours crawling on the dirty floor beside me. He wasn't looking at Mr. Jones or the laughing kids. His eyes were fixed on me.

At first I did not know what to think of the image I was seeing. Jesus had crawled with me all the way over to Mr. Jones. His robe was getting dirty. His hands slid through the same grease and dirt as my hands. He listened to the hurtful and demeaning words of Mr. Jones. Jesus was there at the garbage can as I spit out my gum "like a dog," and he was there crawling with me all the way back to my seat. I was never alone in my humiliation.

As I was spitting my gum into the garbage can, I saw Jesus do something very unusual. When He and I crawled past Mr. Jones toward the garbage can, Jesus reached up and touched Mr. Jones. In the middle of all the humiliation and dishonor Mr. Jones was releasing into my life, God was reaching out to him. Jesus was using my humiliation as an opportunity to touch a very broken man.

What came next was even more amazing. Jan asked, "Is the Lord saying anything to you?" Again, I paused, and waited to hear. The Lord spoke and said, *Garris, what you experienced that day was very painful, but I always provide purpose in the middle of pain. Mr. Jones' actions caused you to pray for him, and I have used those prayers in his life.* For the next fifty years Mr. Jones would be the recipient of my prayers, blessing, and words of prophecy.

That day on the cafeteria floor I was not suffering alone. Jesus was crawling with me through the shame, the dirt, and the public mockery. The first time around, I missed this fact and carried the burden of suffering alone. Now years later, Jesus showed me He was always there with me. I had never been alone. That knowledge has changed how I now view suffering. In our place of suffering, Jesus has promised that He will never leave us or forsake us—ever.

Today, I thank God for Mr. Jones. My experience with a dysfunctional teacher turned out to be a great blessing in my life. Mr. Jones and the trauma he created were unjust and orchestrated from a dark place. But that painful experience was not a wasted sorrow. Years before this beautiful awareness of His proximity, Jesus had already revealed His heart for me and brought much healing. He released the beginnings of the gift of prophecy in my life as I learned how to speak words of forgiveness and mercy over my offender.

The most powerful discovery we will make is to realize Jesus is with us every step of the way. We are never alone. From that realization come the words of life we will speak to people who think they are alone in their shame and humiliation.

Prophetic Principle
THE SOUNDS OF SILENCE

I will never forget one of the most painful experiences in all our decades of ministry. A political spirit had overtaken the hearts and minds of a handful of leaders with whom we worked, resulting in decisions that ran contrary to the heart and methods of God.

These leaders had gathered together to "strategize" during a major transition. When we came to the meeting, it was obvious that decisions had already been made, and the meeting was for the purpose of announcing those decisions. Each leader had a predetermined agenda concerning their future plans. Our presence had become an obstacle to those plans.

Behind closed doors and in secret, they had been trying to figure out what to do with us. The decision-makers were looking for our agreement in order to move forward smoothly and efficiently.

During a break in the meeting, Jan and I went for a walk. We wept for people we cared about who would be affected by this decision. This meeting was not honorable, and we were caught in the middle of the workings of personal ambition. We felt stabbed with grief and sorrow.

We did not want to pick up an offense, however easy it would have been to do so. The Lord had been preparing us for change. For months we knew a transition was near, but we had no visible direction. All we knew to do was to keep our hands open with no agenda. During our walk the Lord said, *Be silent.* When we returned from the break, we obeyed the word of the Lord and remained silent.

After each person in the room took time to speak and address the coming change, Jan and I said nothing. Our silence became obvious to those in the room. At the next break, the person leading the meeting asked to walk with me. He was concerned because I was remaining silent during the group conversation. I told him I had nothing to say at the time. I was there to listen.

We returned to the meeting where the decision was finalized without our input. We were all asked to not discuss the changes with anyone, in order to provide the time needed to lay the groundwork for the plan to be accepted and approved by those in authority. When that was accomplished, the changes would be announced publicly.

I write many years after the events of that day, and can say I am so happy I did not speak. Our silence was used by God to direct us to a good place. Without the silence, I might have become defensive. I could easily have ended up making a way for myself. I certainly could have stirred up trouble, even though the decisions were out of my hands. There is a time to fight—but that was not one of those times.

Silence can be prophetic. An understanding of the gift of prophecy involves more than speech. When an assignment for silence comes, obey God's instruction. Remain silent no matter what is taking place.

From within these seasons of silence will come the course corrections needed to lead you into God's preferred future for your life. The greatest struggle we have in times of silence is trust. In the silence, learn to trust God. He is preparing to lead you to a good place.

Chapter 22
THE CHALLENGE OF IDENTITY

When I lived in Berlin, Germany, I had an appointment to meet with an elderly man at a café in Potsdamer Platz. A mutual friend, who was one of the correspondence secretaries for the first President Bush, arranged our meeting. Potsdamer Platz is an iconic area that was devastated during World War II. After the war, this area became part of East Germany and was occupied by Communist rule throughout the Cold War. Today, it has been rebuilt and is one of the most urbane and architecturally interesting areas in all of Germany.

The man I was to meet was unique. He grew up in Germany before the Nazism of Hitler had fully arrived. When Hitler finally took power, he became one of the Hitler Youth: a paramilitary corps of young boys and girls. Hitler planned to fuel his Nazi war machine with these young people. When World War II was over, this man lived behind the Berlin Wall in East Berlin. His life was surrounded by the gray and drab world of godless Communism. He was now sitting with me at a café living within a free and democratic Germany, in a wall-less Berlin. In his lifetime, he had lived as a German citizen with four very different identities.

After about an hour of conversation, this man made a comment I will never forget. He said, "At this age I am not sure who I am. I began my life as a German. Then I became part of the Hitler Youth. Then I was forced to become a Communist, and now I live in a unified and democratic Germany. Who am I?"

Each of us needs to possess an identity that remains secure and able to move with us through all the changes we experience in life. That identity cannot come from this world—it must come from the greater and more stable reality of eternity. The identity of a follower of Christ is not gained by education, possessions, or by doing the right things. Our identity was purchased by Jesus on the Cross and given to us as a gift.

Peter wrote about this identity in I Peter 2:9: *You are a chosen people. You are royal priests, a holy nation, God's very own possession.* God chose each one of us before we chose Him. At the moment we said "yes" to His choice, He gave us our identity as sons and daughters with a Kingdom inheritance. All of this was given to us before we began living out its reality.

When Paul wrote to the church in Ephesus, he said we are seated with Christ in Heaven at the right hand of the Father. This is not a future position. It is our current reality. This position and its resulting identity is a gift from God given to us the moment we came into relationship with Him through Jesus Christ.

As followers of Jesus Christ, we are described as new creations of God. This "new" status is the result of a radical, supernatural transformation. The word "new" means something that was previously non-existent. Our identity appeared for the first time on earth the day we said "yes" to the offer of salvation in Christ. In that moment, we became new in all aspects.

Our new nature is far more powerful and

transforming than the old one that still lies to us and tries to motivate us through shame. Our new identity is eternally secure and not diminished by whatever we go through on this side of Heaven. That knowledge gives us the peace to endure the labels placed upon us by changing culture, politics, or personal failure.

Over the years, I lost contact with the elderly German man. I am guessing he has passed away. He gave me a real desire to call out identity and destiny in people—independent from the capricious circumstances of this life.

Once we know who we are in Christ, we can endure the upheaval and change that so often visits us. This knowledge will help us prophesy hope to hopeless people.

PROPHETIC PRINCIPLE
REMINDERS OF A FORGOTTEN HISTORY

I was reading Acts 7 where Stephen reminded a group of religious leaders of their abandoned history. This was courageous of Stephen, especially because the existing religious system of his day also controlled the cultural power base. In Stephen's case, his obedience cost him his life.

The same problem of a forgotten history is present today. We have faithful people and church movements who have forgotten the powerful events that crafted their beginnings. Rich in a history of the miraculous power of God, these roots need to be rediscovered and revisited to fulfill destiny. Helping people rediscover their original calling and engage it once again will become the way forward.

If you are someone who reminds others of their history and the great moves of God of their past, the attitude of your heart is as important as the reminder you bring. The message you deliver needs to be wrapped in mercy and grace. Your words will carry an invitation for people to reengage their neglected, God-birthed destiny.

Chapter 23
DIVINE ENCOUNTERS I

During our years in Europe, Jan and I spent a lot of our time traveling in and out of our home base in Berlin. We most enjoyed traveling by train. The pace was relaxing, and the passing scenery was beautiful. On one of our train trips, we were returning from Eastern Europe where we had visited pastors and churches. It was a good trip, but we were tired and ready to get back home.

When we boarded the train, it was almost empty. We made our way to our compartment and slid open the door. These compartments seat six people. They were large enough to stretch out and relax. Glad to have the space to ourselves, Jan and I smiled and settled down to begin our long train ride back to Berlin.

About an hour into the trip, the train stopped at a station in the Czech Republic. As the train began to move once again, we heard a knock on the door of our compartment. I looked up to see a man opening the sliding door and entering. We greeted each other in German, and he took his seat.

I could tell the man was successful. He displayed his wealth in the quality of his clothing and the expensive brand of travel luggage he pulled behind him. His shoes looked handmade.

Right after taking his seat, he began speaking in German. I asked if he spoke English. He said yes and continued speaking in English like it was his first language. For the next few minutes he introduced himself, telling me how successful he was. He shared that he owned several factories in Eastern Europe.

The man continued to talk about himself until it began to feel a bit uncomfortable. The more he talked, the more I realized he did not see how shallow his one-sided status report sounded. After a long while, he finally paused his monologue to ask what I did for a living.

In times like these, I am very careful how I respond. In some conversations, I will hold off providing a specific definition of what I do if I think we need more time to develop a relationship before I say, "I am a pastor." Some conversations end when I reveal my work and calling. This time I said right away, "I am a pastor."

When I spoke those words, it was like a curtain came down and covered the man's face. His expression went from congenial to angry. The atmosphere in our compartment shifted. He spit out the words, "There is no God! Only weak-minded people believe in God!" He went on to vent more statements about God not being real and how foolish we were to believe in Him. As he spoke, he began leaning forward into my space. I was not sure what might develop.

This intense response went on for a few moments. While I listened to the man spew his venom, I was also praying and asking the Lord what I should do. The Lord said, "Tell him I love him and I forgive him."

I raised my hand in an attempt to get this man to pause his tirade long enough for me to speak. He was not used to someone interrupting him. It took him by surprise. When I raised my hand, he stopped speaking and took a breath. I said, "The Lord just told me to tell you that He loves you and forgives you."

I had never seen a response like the one that took place. When the man heard those words, his facial expressions changed in rapid succession. He first manifested a look of shock. Then a stream of tears squirted straight out from his face onto the floor between us. He broke down and began to weep. I looked over at Jan. We were witnessing a man having a divine encounter with God.

After several moments of deep, emotional sobbing, the man was finally able to gain enough composure to speak. Jan and I sat in silence as he began to pour out his heart. He said he used to be a divinity student, training to become a pastor. Because of disappointments in his life at that time, he felt God had turned his back on him, so he turned his back on God. His sorrow about his life had become a deep bitterness toward God. In that moment on the train, God reached through his bitterness and reminded him he was not forgotten, and he was still loved. We were watching the return of a prodigal.

For the next hour, the man shared his heart with us. He held nothing back. He talked about his marriage problems and his struggles in life and business. The man was no longer speaking from behind the veil of his success. He was talking like the hungry prodigal son who came to his senses while examining the contents of a pig's feeding trough. He was getting freer with each confession he made. His entire countenance was transforming before our eyes.

The train approached a town in the eastern part of Germany where the man needed to change trains in order to continue his journey home. He stood and gathered his bags. He thanked us and departed. After he got off the train, Jan and I looked at each other in amazement, realizing we had been honored to witness the miraculous restoration of a broken man.

Then we heard a knock on the window. We looked out, and there below us on the train platform was the man staring up at us. He was waving and smiling. As the train pulled away and his image dissolved in the distance, I was struck by how God was able to relay a single sentence of His love that carried with it the power to transform a life.

When you are faced with great emotion and pain, expressed with anger and belittling words, stop and listen before you respond. Listen for the voice of God. In this moment of waiting, you are making room for God to give you words of life to speak to a broken person.

I had no idea what I would share or how I would respond until God revealed the words to me. I got to see God reach out and restore a lost son. Our role is simply to release what God wants to say. He will be faithful to do the rest.

PROPHETIC PRINCIPLE
SPEAK WITHOUT LEAVING A BRUISE

A friend of mine works with mentally challenged people, some of whom have severe disabilities. One day, he and I had breakfast together to catch up. In the course of our conversation, he described how he and his staff handle violent confrontations. I listened with interest because I know my friend is also a second-degree black belt in karate. I was expecting this highly trained martial artist to tell me how he did some Bruce-Lee-style karate move to subdue an aggressive patient.

He said that because of abuse in the workplace, new ways to handle violent attacks were developed. Each staff member is now trained to not grab a client because grabbing someone could result in bruising, mostly because of the pressure of the thumb. Workers are now taught to touch aggressive clients with only an open hand. They do this by placing their thumb alongside the index finger, forming an open hand. Without the use of the offending thumb, they won't grab a patient and apply pressure that could leave a bruise.

As I listened to my friend, the Lord began to download so much to me about how the Church should engage culture. There is a lot of cultural and theological pushing, shoving, and grabbing taking place. We have all seen the angry confrontations in the public arena of contemporary media. Both sides of an issue can attempt to verbally grab each other, trying to forcefully subdue the opposition with a superior argument. In many cases, these interactions have left bruises.

The writer of Hebrews describes the only thing we can take hold of without leaving a bruise: *hold to the hope that lies before us* (Hebrews 6:18). Hope—not the will of another person or our demand for agreement on a particular issue—is the only safe place to grasp.

When you prophesy, make sure your words offer this kind of hope—a hope that exists beyond your agreement or disagreement. Knowing this hope exists helps us let go of the bruising grip of our determination and reach for something more.

Chapter 24
DIVINE ENCOUNTERS II

Many years ago, I was flying alone from Chicago to Spokane, on my way to meet up with my family. I was happy to be upgraded to first class. I found myself sitting next to a man who was well on his way to being intoxicated. When I sat down, we exchanged greetings and he ordered another drink.

As we droned along at 30,000 feet, he shared with me about his life and business. He had done well on a recent business deal, so I guessed intoxication was his way of celebrating.

After a few minutes, he asked what I did for work.

I said, "I am a pastor."

He smirked, took another sip from his drink and said, "You can't know there is a God!" He went on to add more points to emphasize his take on reality. I just listened. Like I do each time I meet someone like this, I pray. I don't pray out loud, but in the quietness of my heart beneath the audible conversation. I asked God how He wanted me to respond.

I felt led to ask the man a question. I asked, "How much of the world's knowledge do you possess?" He paused. I could tell he was thinking. He did not want to appear too irrational, even at his current level of inebriation. As he considered how to respond, I asked another question, "Would you say you have 50% of the world's knowledge?" He feigned a look of humility and said, "No, not that much."

I continued asking, in order of descending percentages, 40, 30, or maybe 20%? Finally, I said, "Would you be comfortable saying you had at least 10% of the world's knowledge?" That number suited him and his desire to recapture a bit of visible humility. He said, "Yes. I think I have at least 10% of the world's knowledge." I then asked, "You said there is no God. Is it possible that God exists in the 90% of the world's knowledge you have not yet discovered?"

He shouted in a voice loud enough for the surrounding passengers to hear, "That's not fair!"

I said, "Sure it is. By your own admission, you said you don't have complete knowledge. It makes sense that the God you deny could be waiting to reveal Himself to you from the 90% of the world's knowledge you admit you do not yet possess."

The man smiled and said, "You got me!" He ordered another drink, and we went on to talk for the next half hour before we landed.

When we landed, we said goodbye. I went through the baggage claim and on to meet the smiling faces of my family. The incident on the airplane provided a principle for life. God is always positioning us for His greater purpose. My seat assignment was originally in the coach section of the aircraft, but God had someone in first class He wanted me to engage. I was upgraded for a Kingdom purpose.

First class was nice, but being in the larger seat with a better menu was not the reason God put me there. A man was waiting for the words I carried. Obedience in delivering those words to him with honor and grace opened him up to hear the heart of God.

As you go about your daily business, you are always "on call" for God. There will be times when you are obviously being repositioned for a greater purpose and times when it is not so obvious. It is important to stay aware of the possibility of divine encounters so you do not miss them.

PROPHETIC PRINCIPLE
THE SOUND OF JUDGMENT-FREE PROPHECY

I noticed something as I prepared a message on the section in John 8 describing the woman caught in adultery. Most of us are familiar with this passage; the Pharisees brought a woman caught in the very act of adultery and put her in front of Jesus. They wanted to stone her to death for her sin until Jesus invited those without sin to throw the first stones.

> *When the accusers heard this, they slipped away one by one, beginning with the oldest, until only Jesus was left in the middle of the crowd with the woman* (John 8:9).

Something struck me as I read this. Jesus wasn't left alone with the woman; Jesus and the woman were together in the middle of a crowd of onlookers, after the religious accusers had dropped their stones and left the scene. The crowd was now waiting to see what Jesus would do with this woman and her sin.

Jesus gave us a profound picture of how the Church

should live in front of the crowd of culture. If anyone ever wanted to know the difference between an Old and New Testament prophet, this event is a prime example. There will always be people around us who forget we live in a New Covenant with God. God judged everything on the Cross of Christ. Nothing was left out. Although we do experience the consequence of our sin, through confession, repentance, and forgiveness, we can reduce the impact of sin in our life and the lives of other people.

This new way to live our lives was not our idea: it was God's. God sent Jesus not to judge the world, but to save it. He confronted the hypocrisy of the religious establishment in his day, and they departed with conviction in their hearts. Those remaining were an audience of seekers hungry to know the loving God who stood before them.

Yes, Jesus did tell the woman to go her way and sin no more. But the most profound sound a guilty person will ever hear is the sound of rocks of judgment falling from the hands of their accusers and landing at their feet. The only time we should pick up rocks is to build a memorial to God's goodness. The rest of the time, rocks belong on the earth, not in our hands.

CHAPTER 25
REPURPOSED LIVES

My father was a house-moving contractor. During the 1950's and early 60's, when the freeway systems of California were being constructed, entire tracks of homes in the path of a coming freeway would be sold and moved to new locations. Each house was raised from its original foundation, cut into sections, and moved across town.

My father would buy these homes at outdoor auctions. As a young boy, I went with him to several of these auctions. The abandoned neighborhoods where the auctions took place looked like deserted, apocalyptic movie sets.

Once Dad bought a house, he would reassemble it in a different location. It would become a new home for a family who eagerly awaited its arrival.

Recalling my memories of those house-moving days, the Lord downloaded a word to me. He said, "I am re-purposing my people. I am uprooting old ways of thinking and practices that no longer accomplish what I am doing. I am moving them to a new location. I am disconnecting them from what has been familiar and leading them into unfamiliar territory. I want them to trust me as I help them make the move."

For some of you, this move has already taken place. For others, the segmented parts of your life are still in transit, and you are not sure of your final destination. When your life is in a season of significant transition, it is easy to become overwhelmed with the process. It is important to make the passage with trust and rest. These moves are an adventure with God. When He reconnects your life in the new place He has prepared for you, you will have a better understanding of why all of this has taken place.

These transitions are good times to receive a word from God. When I am in a transition, especially when I resemble a vulnerable and dismembered house on wheels rolling across town, my heart is open to words of encouragement, direction, and promise.

Ask God to give you words that express His heart to those in transition. Understanding the Father's heart far outweighs the challenges we experience when we are in route to a new destination.

Prophetic Principle
JUDGMENT AND CONSEQUENCE

Evil and tragedy are orchestrated by Satan, not by your loving Father. Satan was cast into darkness and dwells in spiritual darkness. His plans are formed in darkness. Satan looks for disobedience and rebellion as opportunities to release his evil plans. Don't confuse the consequence of sin with the judgment of God. The consequence of our sin is where the plans of hell come to manifest their deceptive intent.

Satan wants us to doubt the love of God. He wants us to blame God for the pain and sorrow we experience. The chaos, confusion, and evil taking place in world are many times the consequence of our own sin or the sin of others. This is not the judgment of God.

Unless we understand these distinctions, we will end up representing God as a cruel and judgment-happy deity, not a loving Father whose heart is broken when we are broken.

God judged the sin of all humanity on the Cross, fulfilling the demands of His justice. Jesus paid the full price for our rebellion with His death. We are living in a time between judgments—between the Cross and the Final

Judgment of all things.

Understanding our role in this in-between time will craft the tone of our message and the course of our actions. John wrote, *God sent his Son into the world not to judge the world, but to save the world through him* (John 3:17). That same mission was given to the Church. How we unpack our understanding of that mission will define everything we do in His name for good—or for bad.

Chapter 26

WHEN RECOGNITION COMES

There may come a time when the gift you carry is publicly recognized. These times can be challenging because if not handled with humility, they can turn your life in a prideful direction. God may allow your gift to reach a wider audience, but the purpose of a wider audience is for His glory, not yours.

Several years ago, I was invited to speak at a conference. People came to this conference from all over the world. It was an honor to be invited. The organizers introduced me with kind words about my life and ministry.

I didn't always feel successful. At times, I felt alone serving in obscurity with little to show for all my hard work. Many times I wanted to give up and go back to something I could control and count on in more tangible ways. Such mindsets can make a person hungry for affirmation.

When I received recognition at the conference, it was a confirming touch from my Father to me, something I don't take lightly or presumptuously. Later that night, after the conference session was over, Jan and I returned to our hotel room. We had a conversation about the events of the day. I brought up the words of introduction and told Jan what I was feeling. It would have been too easy to let my pride and my desire for affirmation lead me to an unhealthy place. Jan and I prayed, thanking God for the words of honor and recognition and giving them back to God. I gave them back so they could remain in safe hands—outside my ability to manipulate them for self-gain.

Every time I minister the words of God, I am reminded that I have been entrusted with the sobering privilege of getting to partner with the Creator of the universe to bring His love and influence to earth. This is a very empowering and humbling experience.

Knowing and recognizing that He is the source of these experiences will keep the words of recognition spoken over our lives in a safe place—in His hands where they will not be used for any purpose other than for the glory of God and the good of His Kingdom.

PROPHETIC PRINCIPLE
A FAST OF WORDS

At some point, God may ask you to fast from giving prophetic words. These silent times can be for a single meeting or for extended seasons of time. The length and timing of these fasts is up to God.

Once, I was ministering in Central and South America. I was flying from Caracas, Venezuela to Panama City, Panama. I was bumped up to first class. Earlier that day, the Lord asked me to fast from eating during the day in order to prepare for a meeting later that night.

When I boarded the plane, it was the inaugural flight of first-class service for the airline. The airline pulled out all the stops. Excellent food and beverages were available throughout the entire flight. Once I sat down in my comfortable seat, I remembered the commitment I made with the Lord earlier in the day to fast. As entrée after entrée was paraded by me on carts, I kept saying, "No thank you." Eventually one of the flight attendants asked if I was feeling well. I said, "Yes, I am fine." I didn't go into the details.

The desire to prophesy can be like a food-cart that roles by your seat. You want to reach out and take something, but you don't because in that moment God needs your silence more than He needs your words.

I am not always sure why the Lord asks us to remain silent with a verbal gift. I *am* sure that He knows everything taking place and we do not.

I have come to realize these seasons of obedient silence are part of a deeper, maturing work in our lives; they release a greater measure of the Spirit's influence when we do speak at the end of the fast.

When I ended that fast from food, everything tasted better than it had before. In a similar way, when you break the fast of speaking prophetic words, you will have deeper appreciation for the taste of His words in your mouth, and when you speak, they will carry a new authority.

Chapter 27
LET GOD MAKE THE WAY

A few months after planting our first church, I received an invitation to join a gathering of fellow church planters who had also been deployed from Faith Center in Eugene, Oregon. Pastor Roy Hicks, Jr. had sent out many of us to plant churches, so this homecoming was really special.

At the meeting, Roy broke church leaders up according to their congregation size to better address the needs associated with each unique ministry environment. Since I had a total of nine people in my church, I was placed in the group representing the smallest of churches: those under 50 in attendance.

Ron Mehl, the pastor of the Beaverton Foursquare Church, addressed our cluster of small churches. Each Sunday, Ron had thousands of people attend his church services. Being so new and young in this thing called "pastoring," I was blown away that a man of such stature would be speaking to our small group.

I don't remember everything Ron said, but I will never forget two sentences. Ron said, "Resist the urge to make a way for yourself. Let God make the way." At the time, if I could have made a way for myself, I would have tried. I was in a survival mode during those first few brutal months of pastoring, just trying to convince myself to show up again for another Sunday.

Over the years, there have been times when I ignored Ron's advice and tried to make a way for myself. Those attempts usually happened when I was feeling insecure and the unknowns outnumbered the knowns. A few of those times, I embarrassed myself, revealing my insecurity. What redeemed my foolishness and what kept me from repeating it, were those occasions when I remembered Ron's wise words and applied them to the motives of my heart.

Letting God open the doors of opportunity will keep your voice pure and unsullied by the manipulation that can lurk within all our hearts, waiting for a moment of weakness to find expression. Develop your ability to hear the word of the Lord by letting God build your character. Character is what carries your anointing over the long haul. God will be faithful to open doors for your voice to be heard. Let Him be the one who leads you to your audience.

PROPHETIC PRINCIPLE
THE BOUNDARY OF HONOR

I once heard an older pastor say, "If something is public, deal with it publicly. If it is private, deal with it privately." That wise leader was helping a group of us new pastors learn how to deal with disruptions that can take place in a public gathering. If someone is disrupting a church service or domineering a small group meeting, they need to be graciously addressed in public, because the event is being played out in public and impacting the lives of those present.

We are to always be supportive of one another—even when bringing correction. If something is private and limited to only a handful of people, that personal issue should remain in the privacy of that group. On the other hand, if an issue takes place in public it should be dealt with in that public context. The pastor was teaching us the boundaries of honor. This required us to learn the scope of the audience affected by an issue before we dealt with the issue itself.

In a culture where social media immediately releases all the facts without any filter, we can lose sight of the boundaries of honor. When these lines are violated, our voice becomes untrustworthy

Honor will not make what is private, public, and it will not keep private and hidden what should have been handled publicly—whether due to fear or a lack of leadership initiative. Honor should be the filter for how we treat each other.

Chapter 28

WHEN ACCUSATION COMES

As a father in the faith, I find myself viewing the Church from a parental perspective. Most of what I now write and teach flows from the heart of a father. I am protective and inviting—desiring unity, love, and support within the Church. I am grieved when I see competition, division, and accusation.

A couple of hours' drive from our home in Southern Oregon exists a powerful and culture-impacting church. One of the leaders in the relational network of this church invited me to attend a twice-yearly gathering of leaders associated with the global movement that had risen from this ministry.

When I entered the doors of the church, I immediately sensed the honor of God. The worship was sourced from the throne of God. The teaching flowed from the apostolic voices of those who made up the senior leadership team. In the course of a few days, I had an encounter with Jesus similar to the encounter that provided a jump-start for my dead spiritual life in my late twenties.

I came to the meetings as a dry vessel needing to be refilled. I was tired after eight years of spiritual combat, during which time Jan and I helped to build and rebuild our church community. Looking around at others attending the meetings, I saw pastors and leaders from my own family of churches who were walking around the sanctuary with a familiar look on their faces that said, "I want more of this!"

I left the meetings overflowing with a fresh drink of Living Water.

This church, and the movement it has birthed, has taken hits from a variety of different people. Many of these criticisms come from people who have never entered the doors of the church. These accusations are usually fueled by the undiscerning use of social media or church-sanctioned gossip. The scalpel of accusation has sliced and diced this ministry and its leaders without mercy. In the last few years, I have attended several gatherings there, and each time I came away with the same feeling: God is in the house.

I write all of this to say: be careful what you unwisely indict from a distance. Festus gave audience to Paul's accusers: *When Paul arrived, the Jewish leaders from Jerusalem gathered around and made many serious accusations they couldn't prove* (Acts 25:7). What we try to "prove" often comes from the evidence pool of our personal bias and narrow understanding of the real facts. When we finally have our "proof," we gather our supporters to make our case with accusations we cannot fully verify.

Churches and their leaders, like the one I am describing, have always taken hits from those who think they understand all the facts. History repeats itself. These ministries take hits because they are contending for things abandoned by some in the Church. They also take hits from the enemy because they are walking across spiritual frontiers into new and uncharted territories of faith. There is a reality in God's expanding Kingdom: the Spirit will always transport us to new and unfamiliar destinations.

Expansion and change will make some people nervous because a step of faith requires that we leave behind the status quo and accept an invitation to experience something new.

As you develop the gift of prophecy, what you say might be misinterpreted and criticized. You will make mistakes and occasionally stumble while you learn. God will be training you for a lifetime. The process is never perfect. Most people will respond with encouragement. When there is a negative reaction, remain silent until a redeeming word from God forms in your mouth. When that word comes, speak it with humility and integrity. Don't allow a defensive response to take over the sound of your voice, causing you to sound like the very accusations you are attempting to avoid.

PROPHETIC PRINCIPLE
STANDING IN THE GAP

The Lord may ask you to stand between someone who is guilty of a wrong and their accusers who are pointing out their wrong in vivid detail. In this position, some of the most challenging and powerful prophetic statements are delivered without words. Your presence shields the guilty until they can be restored. Your grace confronts their accusers until they can come to their senses and eventually drop their stones of accusation.

This stance is not popular. You may find yourself alone standing against the tide of popular opinion. Your relationships will be tested. Standing between the guilty and their accusers will actually align you with the guilty party in the eyes of the accusers. This is how Jesus lived. He took this position with the woman caught in adultery, with Matthew the dishonest tax collector, and with others labeled as sinners and outcasts.

If you are going to speak for God over the long term, there will come a day when Jesus may ask you to take a similar stance. It is never comfortable, but it is always beautiful when your obedience makes room for mercy to triumph over judgment.

CHAPTER 29
THE POWER OF THE WORDS YOU SPEAK

Several years ago, a friend and I were flying into Eugene, Oregon to minister at a local church. I was piloting a high-performance, single-engine airplane based at the airport in Burbank, California. When we departed from Burbank, the local weather was clear. But from the weather forecast we received, we knew we were flying into deteriorating conditions in Eugene.

After a short stop in Northern California for fuel, we filed an instrument flight plan and took off for the last leg of our trip. Patchy fog and low clouds covered Eugene. As we got closer to the airport, we were number two for landing behind a commercial airliner—a full size passenger jet. We were only a four-seat private aircraft.

We listened to air traffic control and heard the airliner declare a missed approach. The airliner had flown down to the minimum altitude for a safe landing and could not see the runway lighting and therefore had to go around and try again. I turned to the pastor flying with me and said, "Let's give it a try." I based my decision on experience. A large jet aircraft emits a tremendous amount of heat. The heat left behind in the trail of a descending jet can actually change the weather conditions in its immediate flight path and open up the clouds, making a way for the following aircraft to land. That was just what happened with our flight. As we approached landing minimums, we were able to see the runway lights and make a safe and uneventful landing.

That flight is similar to parts of our journey of faith. Each of us will encounter obscuring conditions surrounding our families, dreams, plans, or finances. Some have declared a missed approach because the conditions ahead of them were unsafe for landing.

These missed approaches are not the end of the story. God gives each of us another chance to make a landing. On the day of our flight, after we landed and while taxing to the terminal, we overheard a radio transmission from the captain of the airliner. They were able to land on their second attempt.

When pressured and challenged, we can forget that God is a way-maker when no way seems possible. He is able to alter the conditions along our spiritual flight path and make a way, even using the flight path of those who have gone before us and who had previously declared a missed approach. God will eventually make a way. We are responsible to keep flying in faith and trusting that He is clearing the way before us.

Paul wrote to the church in Thessalonica, *We proudly tell God's other churches about your endurance and faithfulness in all the persecutions and hardships you are suffering* (II Thessalonians 1:4).

When Paul penned that sentence, he used the word *endurance.* Endurance is a composite word created from two meanings, "up" and "to hold." We could read Paul's sentence this way: "We proudly tell God's other churches about your ability to reach up and hold on...." Paul was saying he was proud of the Thessalonian's ability to reach outside their challenging circumstance and take hold of things not yet seen in this realm.

You may be preparing to make a landing into a new season or a new destination. Your flight path may be shrouded by conditions that could cause you to consider aborting your approach. In these conditions, put your trust in the voice of God. He has gone before you. He knows the way. He has a safe landing zone prepared. You will eventually land even if you have to go around after a failed first attempt.

God might give you a prophetic word for someone when they are busy flying by the instruments of faith through dense clouds. The word your deliver might not make sense at the time—like a word describing the heat from a jet engine opening up a way to land when no way seemed possible. But when you faithfully deliver what God has spoken, that word will carry with it the authority of Heaven and will have the potential to open up a way forward when no way is visible.

For I am about to do something new.
See, I have already begun! Do you not see it?
I will make a pathway through the wilderness.
I will create rivers in the dry wasteland
(Isaiah 43:19).

Prophetic Principle
WORDS OF HOPE IN THE VALLEY OF DESPAIR

Mountaintop experiences are not the only times when you learn the heart of God. It is in the sorrow of a dark valley where you have the greatest opportunity to grow in your relationship with Him.

When you find yourself in the deepest crevasse of a dark valley, don't run from the sorrow you find there. Unchallenged sorrow will simply follow you and build momentum. Grief and sorrow can fill your life with bitterness and cause you to live your life as a victim instead of a victor. The only safe place to live is in the heart of God. There He will embrace you and comfort you in your pain. His embrace is where weak and broken people are turned into strong and powerful warriors.

The personal words of hope you hear in a valley of despair will be the same words God will speak through you to those who are walking through their own dark experience.

The story of hope you craft from your season of despair will become the prophetic word of encouragement you speak to people who are walking through their own trauma. When you speak, they will realize they are not alone in the journey.

CHAPTER 30
REDEFINED SEASONS

Several years ago, I booked a cabin along the Rogue River in Southern Oregon for a few days of prayer and study. The cabin was located near the small town of Agness, and I took the long way there, driving through a remote section of the Coast Range along Bear Camp Road. It felt like an expedition.

When I arrived at the cabin, I settled into a daily routine. I spent the mornings in prayer and study. During the rest of the day, I hiked the dirt roads and trails that surrounded my cabin, walking and listening to the Lord.

On one hike, I was walking along a road a hundred feet above the Rogue River. The road was covered with the dark, gray rock used to construct logging roads.

I noticed a white spot in the road ahead of me. Getting closer I could see it was a stone. The stone looked like one of those small stones you would find in a river bottom, where for thousands of years it had been sanded smooth with the passing of time and river grit. The stone was about two inches across. It looked out of place on the dark rock roadway.

Instinctively, I reached down and picked up the stone.

As I held it in my hand, the Lord said, *I have made you a father*. This would sound strange if you knew me since I have two grown children and had been a father for thirty years at the time. But immediately, I knew what the Lord meant. He was making me a spiritual father.

When I got home, I shared the story with my family. I asked my daughter, Anna, to inscribe on the stone the following words, *Agness—Illahe Road, A Father*. The stone sat on my office desk for years. Each time I saw it, I was taken back to that day on the road and the word God gave me.

In the years that followed, I have heard those words, *a father*, from people wherever I ministered. God gave me an upgrade—a greater capacity to receive love and give love, as a father. Fathers and sons speak differently. Whenever I teach or prophesy, much of what I see and say is processed through the grid of a father; I always pray that I will reflect my Father's heart.

God gives each of us a new assignment for each new season of life. The spiritual gifts you release will flow through your life assignment. The content of the words you deliver may even be the same as before, but those words now come through another filter.

Embrace each new assignment, and let your voice reflect the heart of God as you pick up a new mantle for a new season.

PROPHETIC PRINCIPLE
HONORING THOSE WHO WENT BEFORE

One of the tasks of each generation is to honor the pioneers who went before them.

I remember a faithful pastor who found out that an old missionary, who had been used in mighty ways on foreign mission fields, had been forgotten and was living alone in a run-down mobile home. He was ending his days in financial despair. The pastor went to visit the old missionary and saw firsthand what had happened to this man of God.

The pastor returned to the leadership of his church and described in painful detail what he saw. Immediately, they found new housing for the missionary and made sure he was financially secure for the remaining years of his life. They brought honor to the man's life and memory.

Don't forget those who have gone before you because those pioneers cut the path you now walk upon. Someone paid a price for your freedom. When you discover these dear saints, honor them. Honor may be in the form of providing physical resources, friendship, or it may simply be the recognition of their life and contribution.

When we choose to honor others, we honor God. When you honor and invest in those who have been forgotten, you bring them encouragement. This is the heart of God, which is also the heart of prophecy.

CHAPTER 31
YOU BECOME THE MESSAGE YOU CARRY

When you first began to walk with God, you received a message to carry in the form of a prophetic word, a Scripture, or an encounter with God. Such messages act as a compass to help you find your way forward.

As you continue to walk with God, that message will begin to form and transform all aspects of your life. At some point in your process of transformation, you will become the flesh and blood testimony of the message you carry.

When Jesus came to earth in human form, He came as the message of God's love to humanity. He came in this way so we could see and hear what God was like. Jesus was the incarnational picture of God. He took on our physical form and language so we could see and understand His message in our context. In essence, to see Jesus was to see God. To hear Jesus was to hear God. Jesus was modeling for us what a redeemed person could become by living a life of humility and surrender to the will of God.

When Paul wrote to the church in Galatia he said:

Oh, my dear children! I feel as if I'm going through labor pains for you again, and they will continue until Christ is fully developed in your lives (Galatians 4:19).

Paul chose the word "developed" (other translations use the word "formed") which means to give an outward expression to the new nature deposited in your life at the moment of salvation. From this word we get the English word "morph." My wife, Jan, uses a phrase in her Listening Prayer ministry that describes this process: "You are, and you are becoming who you already are." In other words: you are becoming—morphing—into the message you carry.

This message was full and complete when it was first deposited in you. You will take the rest of your life to test its truth and live out its reality. Living out the reality of this message is a Spirit-led process. You are a complete person who now sits with Christ in Heaven. The message you carry flows from that position. Your life becomes an incarnational expression of God's love sent from the throne of Heaven to earth.

Scripture describes you as a dual citizen. You hold citizenship in two realms. One is the citizenship given by the earthly nation where you reside. The other citizenship is defined by your position in Christ at the right hand of the Father. Your citizenship in Heaven is the greater reality. The identity birthed from that heavenly citizenship is the definition of your life.

The by-product of this understanding is the confidence Paul wrote about when he described this morphing process to the church in Corinth:

So all of us who have had that veil removed can see and reflect the glory of the Lord. And the Lord—who is the Spirit—makes us more and more like him as we are changed into his glorious image (2 Corinthians 3:18).

We are being transformed into the message we see with the eyes of faith. This supernatural process of transformation is what you want people to understand as you speak prophetically over their lives.

PROPHETIC PRINCIPLE
DISSATISFIED SEASONS

From time to time you may become dissatisfied. These dissatisfied seasons will not last forever if you remain spiritually healthy. They do need to be addressed because they can lead to a place of spiritual discontent.

There is a positive side to feeling dissatisfaction; it is an opportunity for readjustment and realignment. Dissatisfaction can make you hungry for something new. That new thing is not always a change of location but often a change of heart. Once God has your heart, anything is possible.

When God is processing your dissatisfaction, be careful what you speak. Your emotions and unresolved personal conflict can shade the meaning of what you prophesy. When this happens, people are left with your emotion and not the heart of God.

Always leave them with the heart of God.

Chapter 32

SPEAKING TO AN ANGRY AND FRUSTRATED CULTURE

Forty years ago, I was a young police officer trained as a hostage negotiator. The developing science of hostage negotiation was beginning to be implemented in police agencies across the nation.

Negotiators went into life-and-death situations, hoping to find a peaceful resolution. In those loud and highly stressful scenarios, one of our first tasks was to de-escalate the emotions of the hostage taker. We needed to bring the emotions—and resulting conversation—down to a level where we could begin to find a peaceful resolution. This would only happen if we could establish a two-way conversation.

This de-escalation often took place while a suspect was holding a gun to someone's head or threatening to detonate an explosive device. The suspect's emotions were usually at high intensity. But those emotions often had already developed long before the hostage scenario. Sometime, these events were the result of an entire lifetime of pent-up emotions. In a moment of desperation, the suspects lost their remaining bit of self-control and took a hostage to send the world a message.

When I established contact with the hostage taker, I would begin the process of de-escalation by talking in a barely audible voice. This would cause the suspect to stop yelling and consciously lower his voice if he wanted to hear what I had to say. Our conversation was his only link to the outside world and to freedom.

After we had a few back-and-forth exchanges, the conversation eventually would come down to a volume level where I could hear his demands and ask how I could help. It was amazing to see how that single technique of lowering the volume of the conversation would begin shifting the situation from a potential outcome of death to one of life.

As a culture, we are living in a noisy, anger-driven world. Years of pent-up emotions are beginning to boil over, creating a loud and unhearing audience. God reveals the power of a prophetic word when spoken with the quiet confidence of the Spirit. Increased volume does not gain anyone's attention, nor does it carry added authority.

When a prophetic word is released into a cacophony of human emotion, it will often be the most gentle voice speaking and—in the end—the most impacting. If you are going to be heard as a trustworthy prophetic voice, you will need to take the volume of these heated conversations down to a level where people can begin to hear the word of the Lord. That is when people are set free.

Prophetic Principle
PROPHESYING NEXT STEPS

Hurricanes ravage landscapes and cover communities with widespread damage and sorrow. During terrible storms, people try to find shelter to hunker down and wait for the worst to pass. Almost everything comes to a standstill except the energy released by the storm. Eventually, people will have to emerge from their protected enclosures and reengage life.

The prophetic promise you bring to people trapped in a life storm becomes an invitation for them to step out from their place of hiding and begin trusting that Jesus can get them through all the debris left behind. After these life-altering events, we often hesitate to reemerge, not wanting to leave the security of our protected enclosure. When we finally crawl out after the storm, we are starting all over again because what we knew has been swept away. In these moments of trauma, people need words of hope to move forward once again.

When we are traumatized, we need to know that nothing has the power to extinguish a promise God made before the storm came. God birthed each promise He makes, and He is the one responsible to keep each promise alive no matter what kind of storm blasts through our lives. Our response to the destruction following a storm is to believe the promise is still alive.

When prophesying to people in the aftermath of a personal trauma, help them keep focused on the One who made the promise, not on the storm or its trail of damage. A word of hope will be their place of peace and the substance of their spiritual rebuilding material as they begin again.

Chapter 33
A REDISCOVERED HISTORY

At a time when I did not know I was spiritually empty, I had a much-needed encounter with God. Like so many of us, I had been working for a long season and had failed to replenish the dry places in my life. I needed a fresh encounter with the Spirit. When I say a "fresh encounter," I mean a life-altering experience that causes a person to reevaluate the future direction of their life.

Outwardly, everything seemed to be going well. Our church was maturing and growing. We gathered together in joyful community to worship God and be taught the Word. People were getting saved and set free. Leaders were being raised up. We were financially solvent and had money in the bank. I had nothing I could complain about, but something deep inside me needed a touch from God.

That touch came when I attended a pastor's conference. During that conference, the dry wells of my soul began to overflow with a reconnection to my history. God intercepted me and infused new life into my weariness by helping me revisit my history to discover what I was missing.

These fresh encounters with God's Spirit are critical if

we are going to continue moving forward in the power of God to accomplish His will and finish well. It is too easy to manage our daily work without needing God to show up. True breakthrough can only take place when God shows up in power and does what cannot be done in human strength and will power.

The farther we move away from these Spirit-empowered experiences, the greater the chance will be that our history of God's miraculous work in our lives will become only a legend to future generations.

The first disciples did not let this happen. They lived in the daily demonstration of God's power and presence and continued in that lifestyle until the end of their days. They had no partitions in their faith that relegated the demonstration of God's power to the annals of their recorded history. They lived in a daily dependence on God and the on-going need of an encounter with Him.

If you review the history of the Church over the last century, you'll notice some denominations and church movements that began in a visible demonstration of the Spirit's power now only tell stories of the people who became legends in the early days of their history. Historians ascribe part of this to a sociological process called "Redemption and Lift."

Redemption and Lift starts when we get saved. We begin the process of organizing our lives around Godly principles. These principles begin to affect our character, finances, and relationships. As a result of this transformational process, we begin to rise from the pits of social and economic despair and start climbing higher in the social order. In that rise, we have a tendency to leave behind the very thing that was present at the start of our journey—a dependence on the power of God.

This uplifting process deposits us into a place of respectability. We begin to protect our respectability in order to sustain our newly acquired status in culture. Once our initial needs have been met, we no longer require a miraculous God to show up to meet our future needs because the momentum of our new social status has replaced Him.

The resulting mindset this uplift creates will affect what we do in our private life and in the public display of our faith. Once we arrive at this lifted status, we begin to change our attitudes and language to reflect a false god whose primary goal is to help us maintain our new position in culture. Risk becomes the enemy of our newfound status, and the life of the Spirit that sustained us in the upward journey is now replaced with a dry and empty replica.

As you review the history of revival, it is rare to see a fresh move of God rise up from within existing denominations or church movements. After the first generation of risk-taking, apostolic leadership passes, it is replaced by a maintenance style of leader whose primary role is the survival of the status quo. In the following decades, there may be an external revamping of mission, but at its core nothing has changed. Something still remains in the organizational thinking that makes safety and stability the primary role of leadership. The kind of leader who welcomes the level of risk required for revival, renewal, and a new beginning is not reproduced. As a result, embracing the instability that comes from a fresh encounter with God becomes suspect.

If you find yourself in this place, take heart. Revisit the beginning of your history and the history of the Church, and rediscover what you may have left behind. Reconnect with the faith and passion you once experienced, and you will find a new deposit of spiritual gold that will help you get back on track and rediscover the value of what has been neglected.

Speaking prophetic words is like the discovery of gold. God will reveal a nugget of neglected history hidden under the soil of time. These deposits of gold are discovered each time a new generation digs deep to uncover a fresh deposit of the Spirit. Mining these deposits is what ensures that each generation will finish well.

PROPHETIC PRINCIPLE
THE DANGER OF DISTANCE

Any supernatural ministry of the Spirit can develop a form of spiritual elitism. People who carry these gifts and callings can feel that they are elevated above others and deserve to be treated as such. This kind of separation was never part of the function or definition of any of the New Testament gifts.

Elitism and a resulting separation occur when we attach titles, religious uniforms, and tradition to the function of a gift.

We were given the gifts of the Spirit not to elevate and separate ourselves but to partner with and come into agreement with what Jesus is saying and doing in the lives of people and culture. The evidence that we carry a message from the Spirit is seen most clearly when we deliver it with an attitude of humility and grace.

Chapter 34
DELIVERING HOPE

I have many memorable moments from our years living in Berlin, Germany. One of those moments involved a simple decision to stop and buy some fruit.

After World War II, the Soviets were one of the major powers to occupy postwar Berlin, along with the United States, Britain, and France. Berlin was sectioned off and became a divided city. East Berlin reflected the drab oppression of Communism.

After the Berlin Wall came down in 1989, the surrounding pond of social oppression was drained away leaving the beautiful island of West Berlin standing alone for the world to see. Even into the late 1990's, when Jan and I lived there, this contrast still lingered in city.

In 1998, the city celebrated the 50th anniversary of the Berlin Airlift—an aerial supply line that had been used to bring food and supplies to the residents of isolated West Berlin after the Soviets walled off the city.

The airlift began in the summer of 1948 when the people of West Berlin only had 36 days of food on hand and a small supply of coal. Feeding the two million residents of the city would require 1,534 tons of food and

3,475 tons of coal to be flown into the city each day. To accommodate this massive airlift, flights took off every four minutes, around the clock, seven days a week. These flights continued for over a year. It was a massive and merciful undertaking.

That day in 1998, when I stopped to buy fruit, was like any other in my daily routine in Berlin. I had business downtown and used the S-Bahn to commute into the heart of the city. On my return, my last S-Bahn stop was in our neighborhood of Lictherfelde. Under the train platform was a small kiosk where a vendor sold fruit. As I stood there choosing apples, a man who looked to be in his late seventies approached. When he asked to buy some fruit from the vendor, I could tell by his accent he was an American, so I introduced myself.

We exchanged introductions, and he told me he was in Berlin to attend the 50th anniversary of the Berlin Airlift. He was one of the pilots who flew those daring and dangerous missions. He had been invited to come and be honored for his service to the nation.

Many of the pilots who flew the Berlin Airlift lost their lives flying those missions through dangerous winter weather conditions. Today in Berlin, a monument honors the 39 British and 31 American pilots who lost their lives flying those airlift flights. They were brave men.

One of the stories this pilot shared with me was something called, "Operation Little Vittles." Operation Little Vittles was created as a way to shower the children of Berlin with candy and gum. The pilots put together miniature parachutes, attached candy and gum, and tossed them out of their aircraft as they flew over the city. Hundreds of children would run to the landing zones of these little parachutes for a taste of candy and gum—a very rare treat in post-war Germany.

The Berlin Airlift was such an operational success and political humiliation to the Soviets, that it forced them and the East German Communists to eventually lift the blockade on the city. Shortly after midnight, on May 12, 1949, the blockade of Berlin came to an end (though flights continued for several months afterward).

The mission of these brave pilots strikes me as similar to the mission of the Church. Our communities are walled off behind works of darkness. God has given His Church a calling to bring love, truth, and hope to those who are dying of spiritual malnourishment behind these barriers. Our words and actions are also like those tiny parachutes carrying candy to impoverished children, reminding them that God cares. The food supplies gave their bodies nourishment, but it was the sweet treats that gave them glimpses of hope and a taste of goodness.

When you speak God's word of promise over a life held in captivity to darkness, you are like those pilots who flew in food and supplies to a hungry nation. You are bringing a reminder of hope for eventual rescue. That is the essence of the gift of prophecy.

PROPHETIC PRINCIPLE
WHEN YOU GAIN AN AUDIENCE

People love to hear words of hope. When you begin to walk in the gift of prophecy, your words may create an audience. When you become known as a carrier of hope, people will begin to gather around the sound of your message.

It is important to realize these people are not really gathering around you. They are gathering around the hope of Jesus Christ within you; it is His prophetic presence that is drawing people. You are only a transmitter of His message. Keep that reality in the forefront of your mind when people say kind and supportive words. These comments can be held too closely to the broken parts of your personality that survive by feeding off the need for personal affirmation. This is a critical distinction to make if you are going to remain spiritually healthy over the long haul.

Prior to each new season of growth, you will experience integrity checks that will help you move forward into new dimensions of prophetic ministry. In these checks, you may see ugly parts of your personality emerge; seeing these unseemly parts of our hearts is the first step toward victory. Celebrate this painful revelation because it will keep you from becoming a man-pleaser. Jesus slipped away and passed though the crowds on several occasions. From time to time you may need to do the same.

Chapter 35
PROPHETIC RESOLUTION

A mass shooting took place at a community college in Roseburg, Oregon not far from our hometown. That horrible incident filled our hearts with sorrow. Because I live in Southern Oregon, I know many of the pastors and churches involved in the healing process. A young pastor who is a chaplain for the first responders was there when bodies of the victims were first removed from the scene. He saw things no one should ever have to see.

I met and prayed with some of these church leaders and heard their stories. It was overwhelming. Afterward, I needed to get away and process what I was feeling. I took a long walk along a country road and began to pray. As I walked, the Lord reminded me of something a young man said to me years ago. What made Christianity so appealing to him was the resolution it provided for the pain and sorrow we experience.

Christianity provides resolution for the most challenging and painful things we will encounter in this world—painful events that take place without reason or explanation. Evil has no good purpose. The enemy comes only to steal, kill, and destroy.

I pondered the wisdom of the young man's words. Jesus is God's resolution for all the pain and sorrow of humanity. With Jesus, the resolution for death is resurrection. The resolution for moments of deepest darkness is the brilliant revelation of truth. The resolution available in pits of despair is hope. Each painful thing we experience has a polar opposite resolution of goodness— something only God can provide because it is miraculous in nature.

Every action of Jesus demonstrated the love of the Father. Jesus never attributed untimely death, murder, or tragedy to God. Our response is to believe in God's higher reality of love when evil and chaos speak to the contrary. We are called to respond in faith to the promise of God's goodness.

The Church is a prophetic community. We see things not yet present in our world and speak them into existence. When Paul said he desired that all of us would prophesy, he was inviting every follower of Christ to live from God's Kingdom reality in every circumstance of life. Each of us has the ability to prophesy the hope of a Kingdom resolution into the pain and heartache that overwhelms our cities and our nation.

Our calling is to bring Heaven upon the earth, becoming part of God's redemptive process. We are to speak our words of resolution with wisdom and tenderness and with a Spirit-led sense of timing.

Jesus modeled this for us when He spoke only what He heard the Father saying. When God begins to reveal His heart, you will know it is His voice because He is the one who *brings the dead back to life and who creates new things out of nothing* (Romans 4:17). His voice will carry resolution.

When John shared his revelation from the Isle of Patmos, he described a voice shouting a new reality from Heaven for the earth and its inhabitants:

He will wipe every tear from their eyes, and there will be no more death or sorrow or crying or pain. All these things are gone forever. And the one sitting on the throne said, "Look, I am making everything new!" (Revelation 21:4-5).

John's words will someday be the ultimate answer for the pain and sorrow we have seen in places like Roseburg, Oregon and in many other places across our world when senseless acts of evil happen. God's goodness will be the ultimate reality for every hurting heart in every circumstance of life. This resolution is the message we carry. Speak words of hope, and trust in the goodness of God to prevail.

PROPHETIC PRINCIPLE
WHEN A WORD WAITS IN TIME

Have you ever given a prophetic word and nothing happened? A word may linger for years in the life of a person or within a cultural context, appearing to have found no fulfillment. When nothing seems to happen, you will understand how the men and women in Scripture felt when they prophesied about things they would not see fulfilled for years or even in their lifetime.

Heaven's timing is different from earth's timing. Heaven is an environment that is immediate and now. Heaven doesn't have a future because it is eternal. When a word from Heaven enters the realm of earth, it comes carrying that eternal essence. As a word arrives, it does not submit to our timeline but waits for Heaven's timetable in concert with the heart and plan of God. This is why some words require a season of waiting. God is always doing more than we can see or understand.

As God orchestrates the timely delivery of a word, your job is not to make it happen. In the waiting, pray for hearts to open. Intercede for situations to change. Worry about nothing, but pray about everything. God will not delay. He will confirm and perform His word.

If you get to see a prophetic word finally germinate and bear fruit in your lifetime, you will begin to understand the reason for the wait. You will see how the supernatural hand of God was at work. You will learn to love His wisdom and His timing. This is the fruit of waiting and trusting.

A Final Word

When Paul said he wished we could all prophesy, he was speaking about a preferred future where each of us would come to realize our God-given potential to speak His words in His name.

Your voice has the power to create or destroy. The Kingdom you represent brings life into dead places. Your assignment is to call into being things that do not yet exist and give life to things that have died. This is a beautiful calling: a calling of God-empowered words and action.

Press into this essence of the gift of prophecy. Let God flow through you to express His heart with your unique voice. When He released a word from Heaven, He did so knowing it would pass through the filter of your life experience and personality. Get comfortable with that reality because it will help you speak with the unique sound of your own voice. God loves to hear your voice carry His words of hope and direction to a world that desperately needs to hear a message of love and redemption.

Ministry Contact:

Garris Elkins
Prophetic Horizons
P.O. Box 509
Jacksonville, Oregon 97530
GarrisElkins.com

Other books by Garris Elkins
(available on **amazon.com**):

A Good Place
God-Whispers
The Leadership Rock
Prayers from the Throne of God
Thoughts to Leave Behind

Made in the USA
San Bernardino, CA
19 March 2017